REED'S
Skipper's Handbook

by

MALCOLM PEARSON
Yachtmaster

AN AIDE-MÉMOIRE
AND
QUICK REFERENCE GUIDE

LONDON • BOSTON

NAUTICAL PUBLISHERS SINCE 1782

First Published 1993

Thomas Reed Publications Limited,
Thames Wharf Studios,
Rainville Road,
London W6 9HA

Tel: 071 385 3344 Fax: 071 386 0911

Acknowledgements

Crown Copyright.
The figures on pages 19, 20, 21, 53, 60, 63, 71 and 78 are based upon or are reproduced from Admiralty Charts or publications with the kind permission of the controller of Her Majesty's Stationery Office.

To the Editor of Practical Boat Owner, my thanks for permission to reproduce material previously published in the magazine.

Thanks to Reed's for pages 54-55, their system is better than mine.

My special thanks and gratitude go to my friends and fellow yachtsmen, David Poole and John Harrison for their advice and encouragement and for their time spent in reading and checking the text, and last, but by no means least, to my wife Sherrie whose support and tolerance made this book possible.

Important Legal Note

ISBN 0 947637 43 5

Original Drawings by Sherrie Pearson

Illustrations by Barbara McGavin

Printed in Great Britain by Barwell Colour Print Ltd.

Bound by Bocardo Press, Didcot

Preface

As its title suggests, this little book was conceived as a memory aid rather than a comprehensive manual of navigation. Nevertheless, it is one which provides all the essentials in brief and with its lucid text, simple illustrations and step-by-step procedures is a reliable source of information for the student and budding yachtsman.

More experienced sailors, who have already mastered the basics of navigation may still find themselves in need of occasional prompting. This handy pocket-sized book does just that. It may be kept close to hand and consulted to find the answer to most of the problems that are likely to present themselves during a coastal passage.

Dedicated to Jack -
my evening star

May he never lose his way

Contents

REED'S

Skipper's Handbook

The network of lines on a globe of the world are used to define position on its surface. The horizontal lines are called Parallels of Latitude and the vertical lines which converge at the Poles are Meridians of Longitude *Fig 1*. Latitude is measured vertically along a meridian from 0° to 90° either North or South of the Equator *Fig 2*. Longitude is measured horizontally around the equator from 0° to 180° either East or West of Greenwich Meridian *Fig 3*.

There are 360 degrees in a circle, 60 minutes in a degree, and 60 seconds in a minute and every place on the surface of the earth has its own parallel of latitude and meridian of longitude which can be accurately defined by using these geographical co-ordinates.

In coastal navigation it is usually adequate to define a position to the nearest minute, but if greater accuracy is required, tenths of a minute may be quoted as well.

Traditionally, Latitude is always given first followed by Longitude.

i.e. Bishop Rock 49° 52′.3N 6° 26′.7W

Charts are also overprinted with a lattice of Latitude and Longitude but on charts drawn to Mercator's projection (a method used to portray the spherical world on a flat chart) the meridians are made parallel to each other and so, in order to preserve the shape of the land, the North/South distance between successive parallels of latitude is progressively increased in proportion toward each Pole.

Latitude and longitude

1

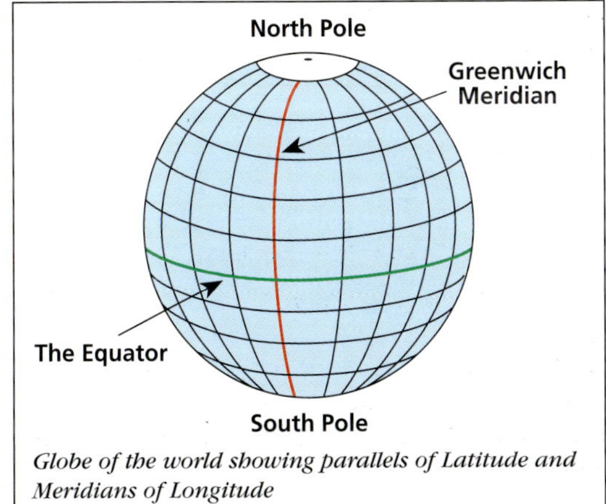

Globe of the world showing parallels of Latitude and Meridians of Longitude

2

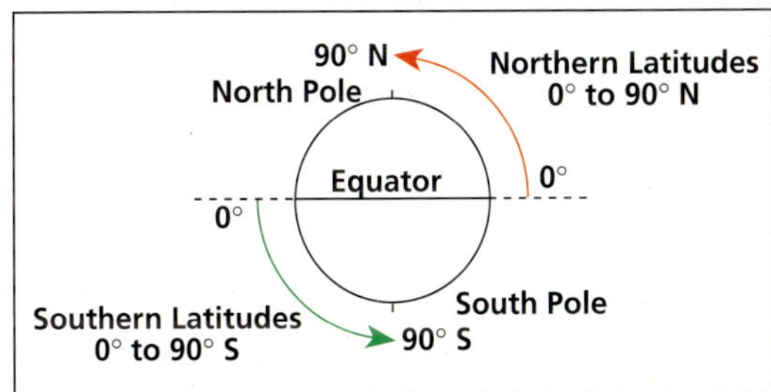

3

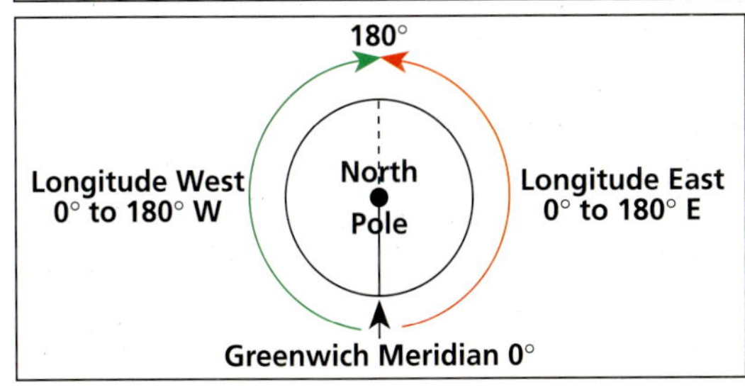

Measuring distance

4

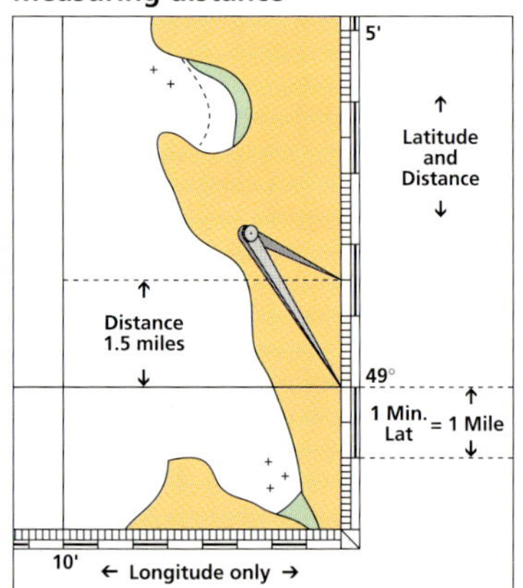

Because of the fixed relationship between the distance which separates any two positions on the Earth's surface and the angle between them as measured from the centre of the earth, navigators use a unit of distance which is related to angle – the Nautical Mile.

By international agreement the length of a nautical mile has been fixed at 1852m (6076ft) which is a distance on the surface equivalent to one minute of arc subtended at the centre of the Earth. The nautical unit of speed is the Knot, which is equal to one nautical mile in one hour.

A scale of distance is provided by using the latitude scale at the chart sides where one minute of latitude is equal to one nautical mile but, because this scale gradually changes as latitude increases - *see page 2* - distance must only be measured on that part of the scale adjacent to the area of the chart being used *Fig 4*.

Plotting

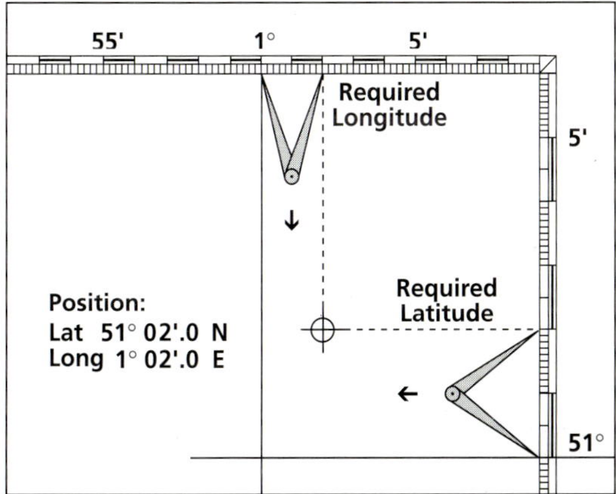

Position on Earth's surface can be expressed in terms of Latitude and Longitude.

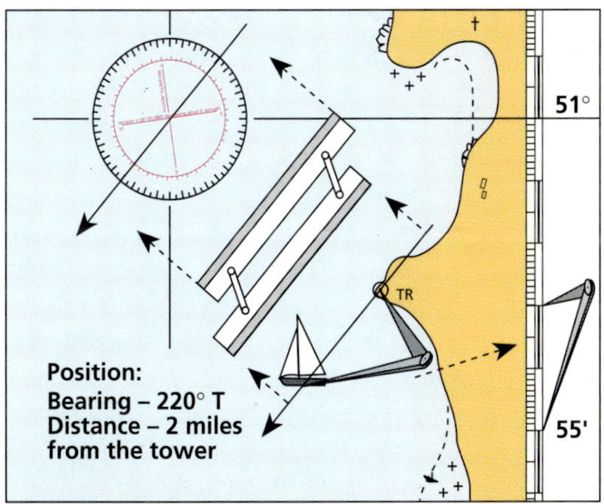

In coastal navigation the position of a vessel is more often identified by its bearing and distance from a charted place or feature.

Direction on the surface of the Earth is measured clockwise from North using 360° notation. Charts are oriented to True North but the magnetic compass which is used to determine direction points to Magnetic North. The angular difference between True and Magnetic North is called Variation and this may be either Easterly or Westerly depending upon the *vessel's geographic position Fig 1*.

The magnetic compass is subject to interference from within the boat caused by nearby electrical equipment or ferrous masses which deflect the compass card away from magnetic north. This effect is called Deviation and may be Easterly or Westerly depending on the *vessel's heading Fig 2.*

The difference between a Compass bearing and a True bearing is the sum of Variation and Deviation and is called the 'total error'.

A navigator must convert a course steered by Compass into a True course in order to draw it on the chart, and must convert the True bearings taken from the chart into Compass bearings to steer a course by (*see pages 10 & 11*).

Variation not only differs from place to place, but also from year to year. The figure indicating local variation at the date a chart is published is usually printed across the compass rose together with the rate of annual change. i.e.

Variation 5°.55′ W (1985) decreasing about 5′ annually.

Therefore, if you were using this chart in 1993 the variation to apply would be 5°.15′W (or just 5°W as it is usual to round variation to the nearest full degree).

Variation and deviation

1

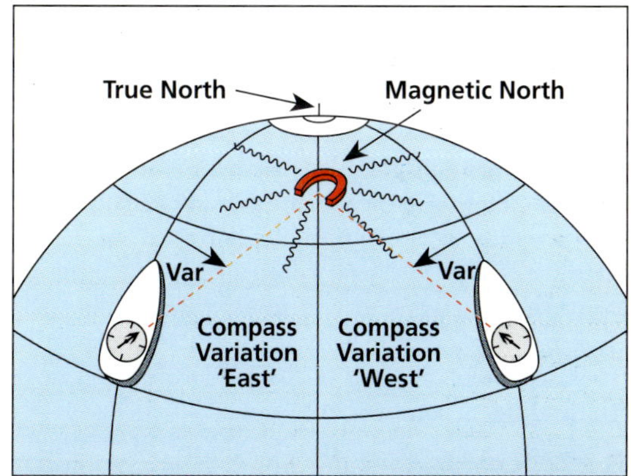

*A Magnetic Compass points toward Magnetic North – **not** True North. Variation is the angular difference between them.*

2

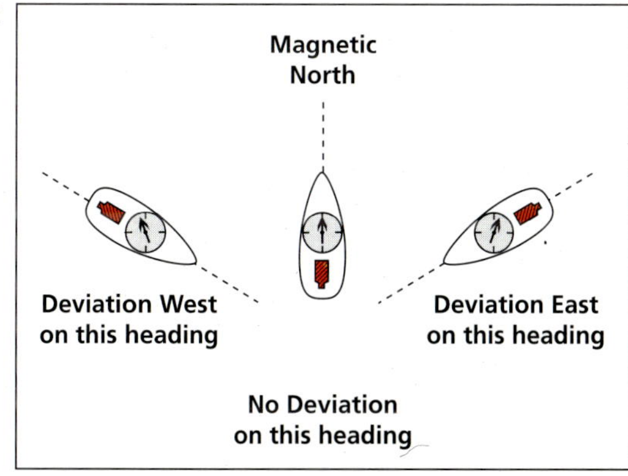

This boat's engine is influencing the compass card. Each time the course is altered the position of the engine in relation to the compass changes and so does the deviation on that heading.

Checking the compass

Compass deviation is no problem in itself provided that the error for each heading is known and allowed for.

Steering Compasses should be positioned where they can easily be seen by the helmsman but as far away as possible from the influence of ferrous masses and electrical equipment. After siting, every steering compass should be checked by a qualified compass adjuster who will adjust the compass and then prepare a deviation card for any residual error. This deviation card shows the deviation for each of 16 headings around the compass *Fig 3*.

It is both reckless and potentially dangerous to rely on an uncorrected compass, so if for any reason its deviation is unknown, you should run your own check on it.

A rough guide to the deviation on a single course can be obtained by standing in the stern - well away from all magnetic influences - and sighting the mast and bow *Fig 4* with a hand bearing compass. Compare the reading obtained with that shown by the steering compass and any difference will be the deviation on that heading.

If the same procedure is repeated for each of the headings shown on the card in *Fig 3*, you can produce your own deviation card for the compass in question.

Swinging the compass

3

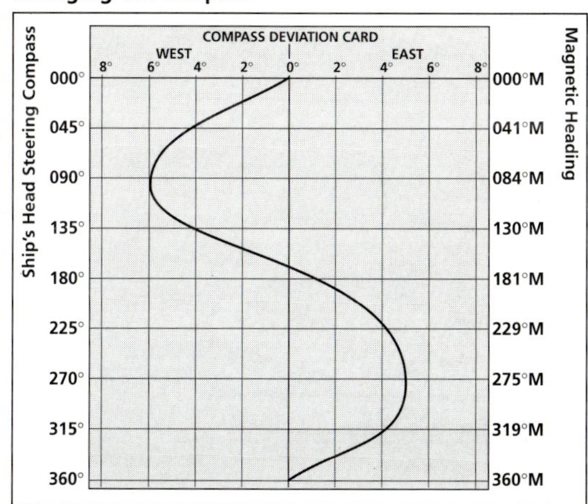

Deviation is measured for a given ship's heading - not for a magnetic course - each deviation has been applied to the ship's head by compass to give the equivalent ship's head magnetic (see compass conversion, pages 10 and 11).

4

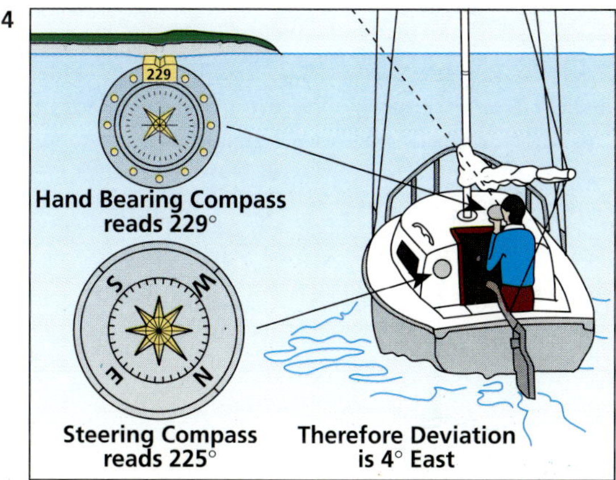

Compass Conversion

True bearing to compass bearing

To convert a TRUE course into a Compass course apply correction for Variation and Deviation in the sequence shown.

If the error is -

West – *add* the angle.
East – *subtract* the angle.

True°	Var^N	Mag°	Dev^N	Comp°

→ E –
W +

1 Apply Variation to the TRUE course to obtain the Magnetic course.

2 Apply Deviation to the Magnetic course to obtain the Compass course.

NOTE The appropriate Variation is obtained from the chart in use and Deviation is taken from the Deviation card belonging to the steering compass being used. *(See pages 6 and 8)*

Compass bearing to true bearing

To convert a Compass course into a TRUE course apply correction for Deviation and Variation in the sequence shown.

If the error is -

East – ***add*** **the angle.**
West – ***subtract*** **the angle.**

Comp°	Dev^N	Mag°	Var^N	True°

E + → W –

1 Apply Deviation to the Compass course to obtain the Magnetic course.

2 Apply Variation to the Magnetic course to obtain the TRUE course.

NOTE Hand Bearing Compasses which are used in locations away from ferrous metal and electrical fields are deemed to be free of Deviation error therefore bearings taken with them are 'Magnetic' and only require correction for Variation to convert them to TRUE.

Cause and effect

Leeway is the angle between the direction of the boat's heading and the direction in which she is actually moving through the water as a result of being blown sideways - off course - by the wind.

The amount of leeway experienced varies from boat to boat depending upon hull design, draught, windage of superstructure or rigging, and also upon the 'point of sailing'. Leeway is at its maximum when sailing close hauled and at its minimum when running downwind or motoring head to wind.

In the diagram, A-B is the boat's course (the direction in which she is pointing). If no other influence affects that course she will eventually arrive at B but, with wind on the port beam the boat is being blown to leeward - downwind - of the course steered and in fact moves along line A-D although at all times her heading has remained parallel to A-B. The line A-D is therefore the boat's track through the water and the angle that A-D makes with A-B is the 'Leeway Angle', for which an allowance must be made if serious errors in estimated position are to be avoided.

Wind from Port side:
Water track is *greater* than the heading

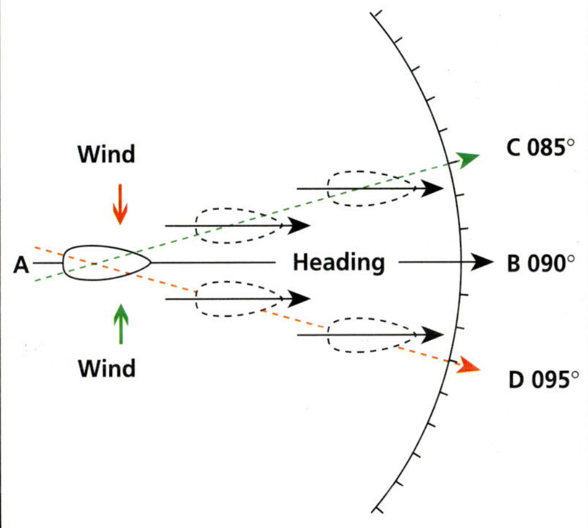

Wind from Starboard side:
Water track is *less* than the heading

Making allowances

Because boats and conditions vary so widely there are no sophisticated ways of assessing leeway. The various methods that are employed are all little more than guesswork, and it is not uncommon for some skippers to merely apply an arbitrary 5° allowance whatever the boat or conditions - a practice that cannot be recommended for obvious reasons.

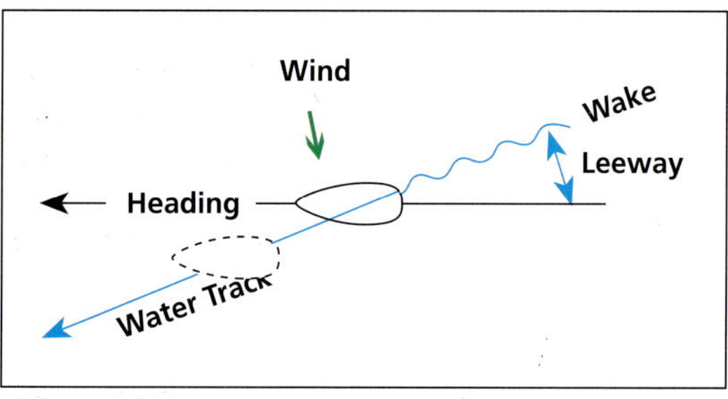

It is often possible to estimate leeway by reference to buoys or shore marks but perhaps the simplest method is to look aft and estimate the angle between the boat's fore and aft line and its wake.

Unfortunately, whilst this method produces quite reasonable results, just when leeway is likely to be at its maximum - when sailing close hauled in a lumpy sea for instance - the wake is not always very clear, and so at times like this or whenever there is doubt, always try to be upwind (and uptide) of your destination especially when approaching the coast at right angles.

When converting a TRUE course taken from the chart into a course to steer by compass, make an allowance for leeway that is anticipated by applying the appropriate angle to **WINDWARD** of the TRUE course in the following manner:-

Wind from Port – ***subtract* the angle.**

Wind from Starboard – ***add* the angle.**

(see Course to Steer page 22)

When converting a course that has been steered by compass into a TRUE Course to be plotted onto the chart, make an allowance for leeway which is estimated to have occurred by applying the appropriate angle to **LEEWARD** (downwind) of the TRUE course steered in the following manner:-

Wind from Port – ***add* the angle.**

Wind from Starboard – ***subtract* the angle.**

(see Establishing Position page 30)

The effect

All vessels afloat in tidal waters are affected by tidal streams - the horizontal movement of the sea caused by the rise and fall of the tide.

The direction in which the stream is moving is called the SET, the speed at which it moves is the RATE, and the distance the stream (and everything afloat in it) travels in a given time is called the DRIFT i.e.

SET 090°, RATE 2 Knots = an Eastward DRIFT of 2 nautical miles in one hour *Fig 1.*

1

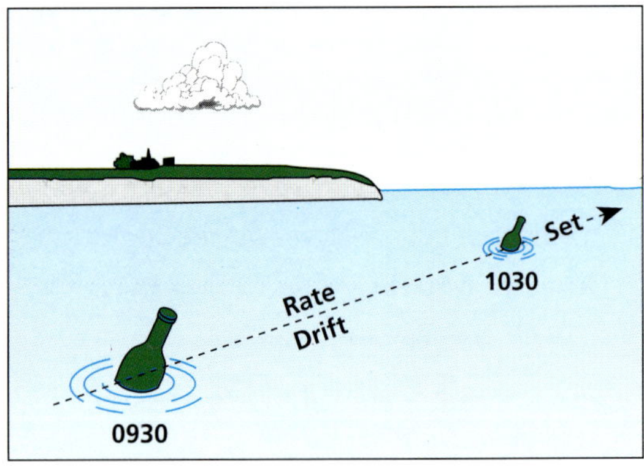

The set of the tidal stream relative to the boat's heading may assist progress *Fig 2* or hinder it *Fig 3* but it may also push you off course *Fig 4* in which case it becomes necessary to compensate for 'lateral drift' by steering up into the stream slightly and 'crabbing' along the desired course. The precise angle at which the boat must be steered to do this is determined by the speed of the boat through the water and by the rate and set of the tidal stream *(see Course to Steer page 22).*

2

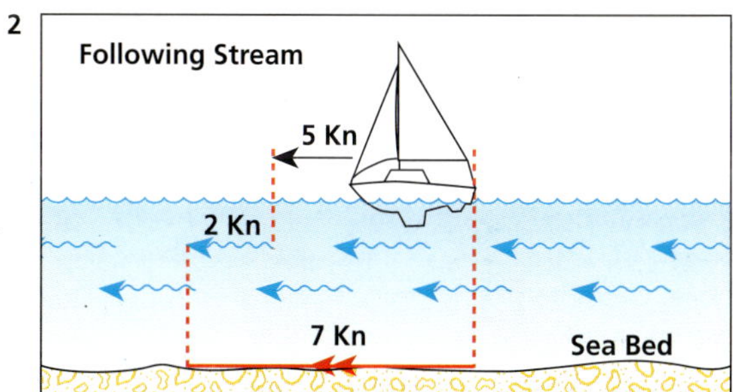

Speed over ground = Boat speed + Tidal Stream

3

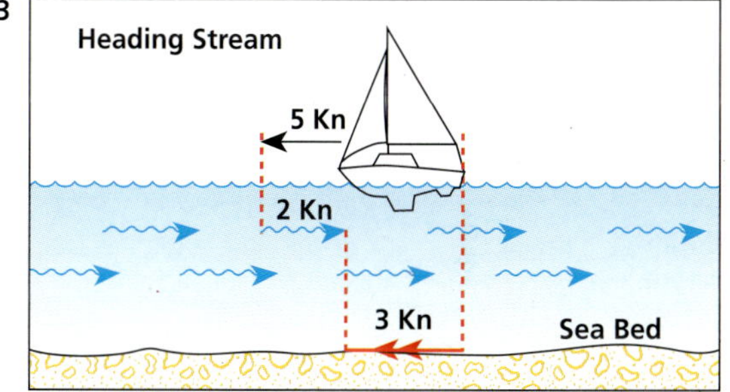

Speed over ground = Boat speed - Tidal Stream

4

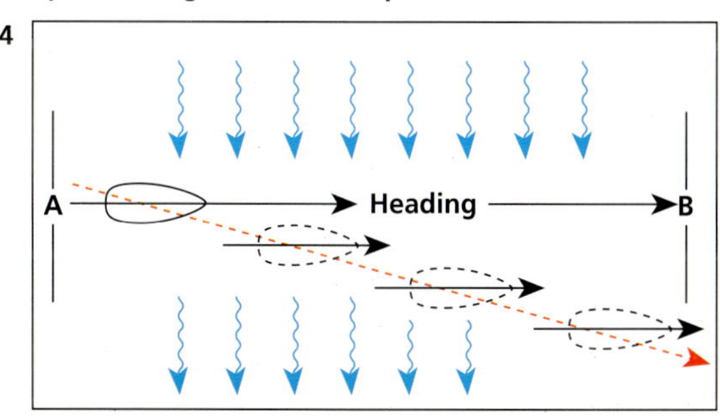

Tidal Stream setting vessel "off" course to starboard

Sources of information

Information concerning tidal streams can be found on Admiralty Charts and in Tidal Atlases.

Positions where tidal streams have been measured are marked on Admiralty charts by a letter within a diamond. An associated table shows the set and the Spring and Neap rate of the streams at these positions for each hour before and after HW at the standard port *Fig 1*.

Tidal Atlases have a separate page for each hour before and after HW at a standard port upon which the set of the tidal stream is depicted by arrows with figures alongside to indicate the mean rate in tenths of a knot at Springs and Neaps *Fig 2*.

To use either method you must first obtain the time of HW at the relevant standard port and pencil it in on chart or atlas together with the times +/- HW as required. You can then see at a glance what the tide is doing at any particular time.

Nautical almanacs and the excellent Tidal Atlases produced by the late Michael Reeve-Fowkes also provide the same information in different forms and both include full instructions for their use.

Chart

1

Tidal Streams referred to HW Dover

Hours	(A) 50°42'3N 0 26'5E			(B) 50°53'0N 1 00'6E			(C) 51°01'0N 1 10'0E			(D) 51°09'7N 1 27'8E			(D) 51°03'0N 1 40'0E		
	Dir	Rate *(kn)* Sp	Np	Dir	Rate *(kn)* Sp	Np	Dir	Rate *(kn)* Sp	Np	Dir	Rate *(kn)* Sp	Np	Dir	Rate *(kn)* Sp	Np
Before HW 6	248	0.8	0.4	211	1.6	0.9	224	0.9	0.5	212	2.2	1.2	220	1.7	0.9
Before HW 5	067	0.5	0.3	211	2.1	1.2	239	1.0	0.6	213	2.2	1.2	220	2.8	1.6
Before HW 4	068	1.9	1.0	211	1.8	1.1	235	1.1	0.6	216	1.9	1.1	220	3.5	2.0
Before HW 3	068	2.6	1.5	211	0.9	0.5	242	0.6	0.4	228	1.3	0.8	220	2.8	1.6
Before HW 2	068	2.3	1.3	*S l*	*a c*	*k*	*S l*	*a c*	*k*	*S l*	*a c*	*k*	220	1.2	0.7
Before HW 1	068	1.2	0.6	031	0.8	0.5	052	0.6	0.3	032	1.2	1.7	040	0.8	0.4
HW	067	0.1	0.1	031	1.5	0.8	049	1.2	0.7	038	2.0	1.2	040	2.5	0.1
After HW 1	248	0.9	0.5	031	1.9	1.1	049	1.3	0.7	039	2.3	1.3	040	3.4	1.9
After HW 2	247	1.4	0.8	031	1.7	1.0	156	1.0	0.5	034	2.2	1.2	040	2.9	1.6

Tidal Atlas 'Chartlets'

2

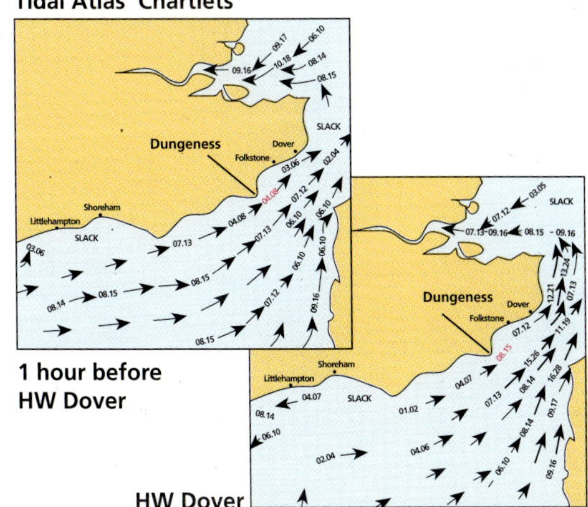

1 hour before HW Dover

HW Dover

Interpolation of rate

The rate of tidal streams is assumed to vary with the range of tide at the standard port. For times **between** full springs and neaps you must interpolate between the rates given in order to plot accurate tidal vectors when estimating position or finding a course to steer and this can be done by using the computation of rate graph supplied with the atlas *Fig 3*, or arithmetically with the formula:-

$$\frac{\text{Range of tide for day}}{\text{Spring range of tide}} \times \text{Spring rate of tidal stream}$$

Remember too that if your course passes through an area marked by more than one tidal diamond or falls between two tidal stream arrows, it is also necessary to estimate what the rate is likely to be in the area between these positions *Fig 4*.

4

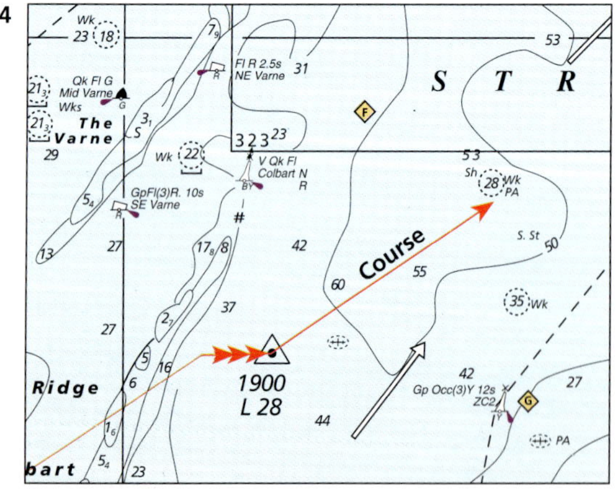

3

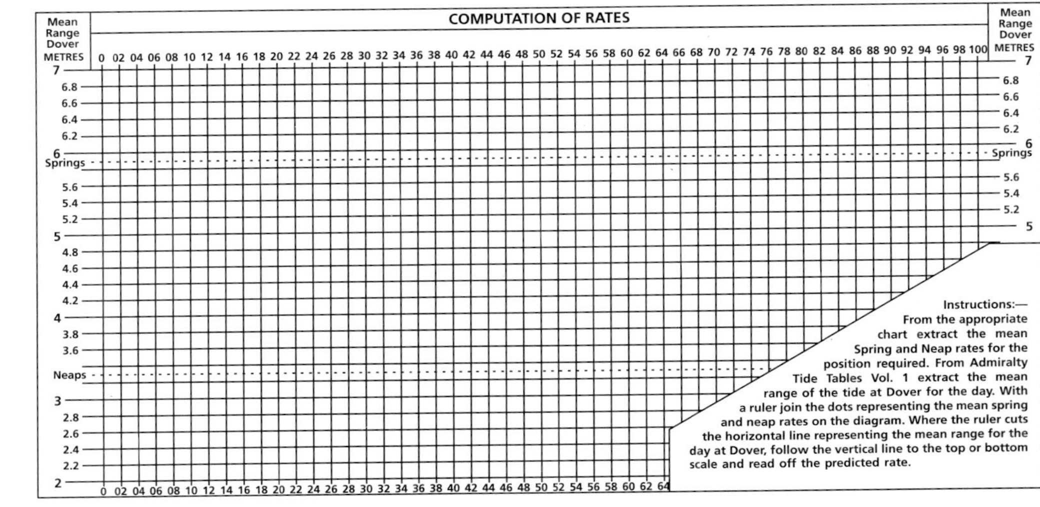
COMPUTATION OF RATES
Mean Range Dover METRES
0 02 04 06 08 10 12 14 16 18 20 22 24 26 28 30 32 34 36 38 40 42 44 46 48 50 52 54 56 58 60 62 64 66 68 70 72 74 76 78 80 82 84 86 88 90 92 94 96 98 100
7 6.8 6.6 6.4 6.2 6 5.6 5.4 5.2 5 4.8 4.6 4.4 4.2 4 3.8 3.6 3 2.8 2.6 2.4 2.2 2
Springs
Neaps
Instructions:—
From the appropriate chart extract the mean Spring and Neap rates for the position required. From Admiralty Tide Tables Vol. 1 extract the mean range of the tide at Dover for the day. With a ruler join the dots representing the mean spring and neap rates on the diagram. Where the ruler cuts the horizontal line representing the mean range for the day at Dover, follow the vertical line to the top or bottom scale and read off the predicted rate.

To find the course over a short period

1 On the chart *Fig 1*, plot the required ground track from start to finish.
A-B

2 From the starting point, plot the set of Tidal Stream using units of length equal to its rate in knots.
A-C

3 With dividers centred at the end of the Tidal Stream Line **(C)** and set to a radius equal to the anticipated speed of the boat through the water, swing an arc to cut the ground track **(D).**

4 A line connecting the end of the Tidal Stream Line and the cut just made is the required Water Track.
C-D

5 Measure the TRUE bearing of the water track and to **WINDWARD** of it make an allowance to offset any leeway expected. This is now the course to steer TRUE.
C-E

6 Apply variation and deviation to this course as necessary to obtain the course to steer by compass *(see page 10).*

NOTE Vector triangles are usually drawn for periods of one hour, although longer or shorter periods may be used if appropriate. Whichever time scale is chosen, it is essential to use the same ration for each vector i.e. one hour of tidal drift with one hour of boat speed.

1

Leeway Allowance
(applied to prepared course to steer)

Wind from **Port** side
Subtract the angle

Wind from **Starboard** side
Add the angle

Compass Conversion
(applied to proposed course to steer)

Variation/Deviation **East**
Subtract the error

Variation/Deviation **West**
Add the error

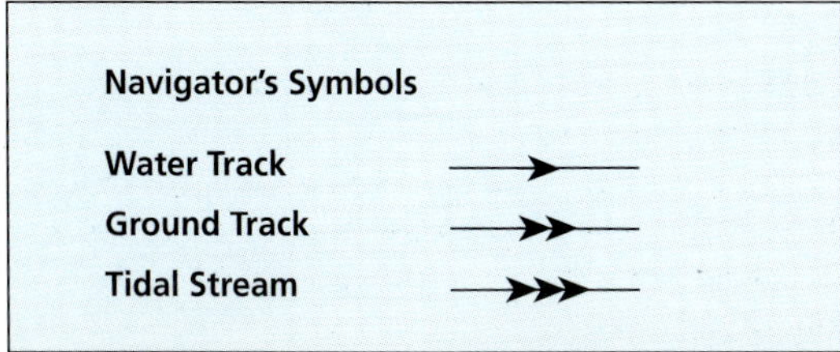

Tidal streams and longer passages

Tidal streams usually take one of two main forms: **Rectilinear,** where they flow in one direction for half a tide and then reverse to flow in the opposite direction with a period of slack water at the turn of the tide *or*

Rotary, in which the stream changes direction from hour to hour, often without a period of slack water.

To find the course to steer across a channel with opposing streams, first work out how long the passage will take *Fig 1*. To do this measure the distance across - 60 miles - and divide this figure by the anticipated boat speed - 6 knots. Time to cross = 10 hours. Next, add up all the Westerly and then the Easterly streams for each hour and subtract one from the other.

Plot the balance of tide as a vector from the starting position *Fig 2* and lay off the distance to travel from the end of it. Apply leeway, variation and deviation in the usual way to obtain the course to steer.

To make a crossing with Rotary streams *Fig 3* find the distance and crossing time as before but this time plot tidal vectors for each hour and link them as shown. From the end of this chain lay off the distance to travel and apply leeway, variation and deviation to obtain the course to steer *Fig 4*.

Rectilinear tidal streams

1

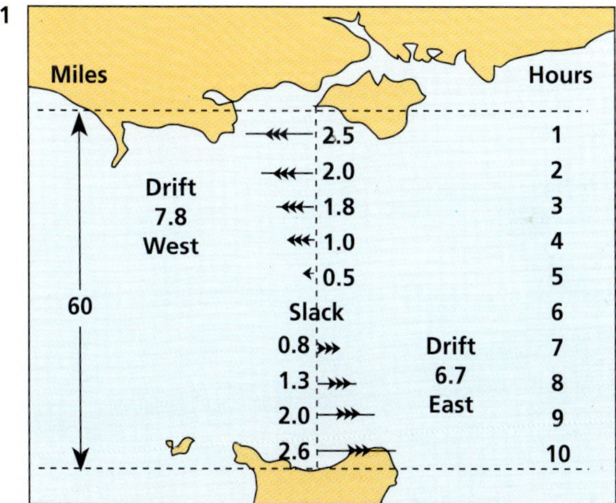

Distance to go ÷ Estimated Speed = Time to Cross

2

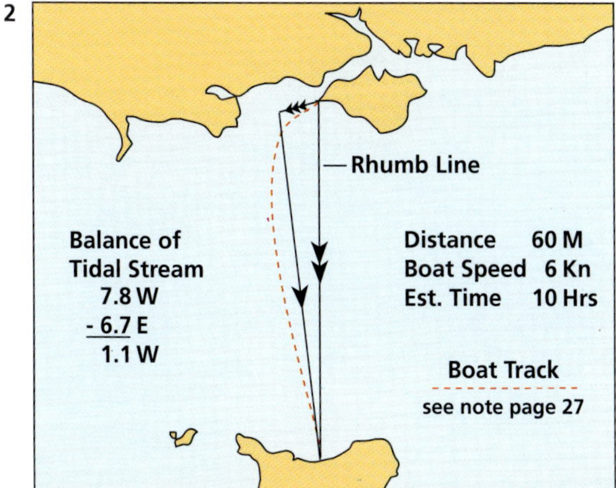

Rotary tidal streams

3

Distance - Miles

Time - Hours

1
2
3
4
40
Boat Speed 5 Knots
5
6
7
8

4

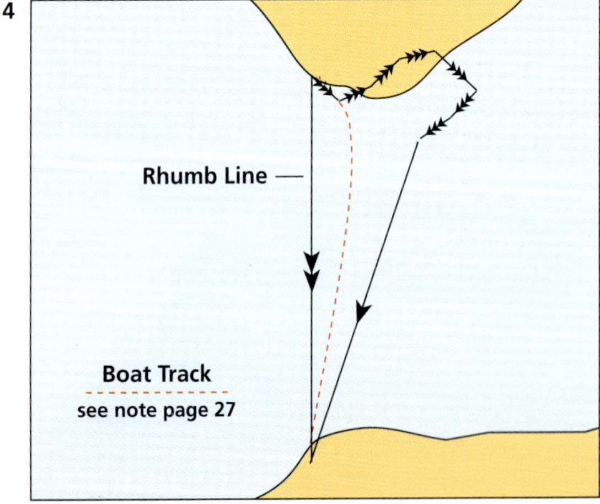

NOTE Steering a single course across an ebb and flood tide will take the boat well away from the required rhumb line so make certain that no dangers exist on either side. Plot an EP for every hour and work out a new course to steer each time that the distance to your destination is halved.

The alternative is to shape a separate course to steer for each hour of tidal stream. This will keep the boat on or close to the rhumb line but depending upon wind direction, a sailing vessel may find it difficult to achieve some of the headings required *Fig 5*.

5

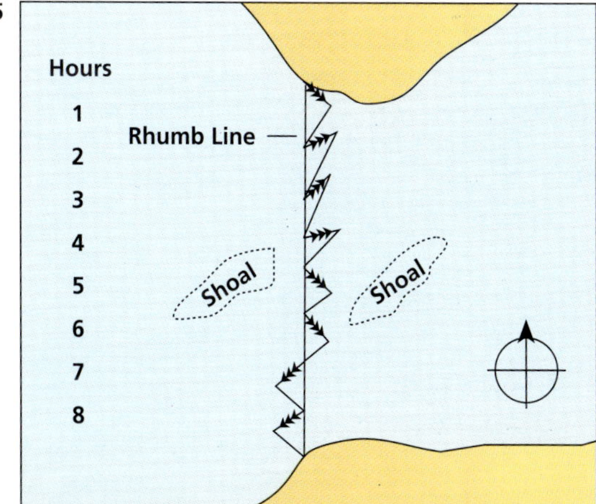

Tidal Streams along the coast

The strength and speed of tidal streams inshore is determined to a large extent by the geography of the area. Irregularities of the coastline and obstructions to the flow caused by ridges or shoals on the sea bed combine to affect the pattern of behaviour of the streams and sometimes give rise to races, overfalls, and tide rips *Fig 1*.

Tidal streams running parallel to the coast will run more strongly past headlands **(A)** and less so within bays into which they have a tendency to set, sometimes with a 'counter current' or back eddy developing in the tidal lee of the headland **(B)**.

A tidal stream which is obliged to flow through a narrow channel or converge with a stream from a different direction may speed up to form a race against which passage is virtually impossible, and during adverse weather these areas are best avoided altogether **(C)**.

A ledge or steep-faced shoal on the sea bed may deflect a tidal stream upwards causing broken water or 'overfalls' on the surface which in strong wind over tide situations can be very dangerous **(D)** and *Fig 2*.

1

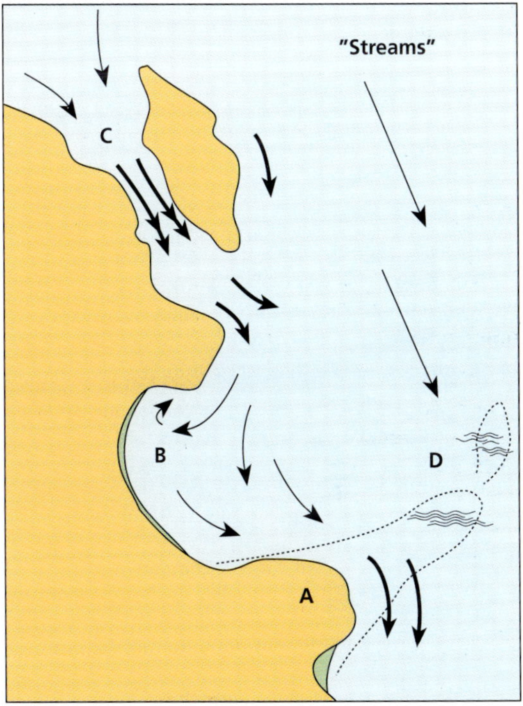

"Streams"

C

B

D

A

2

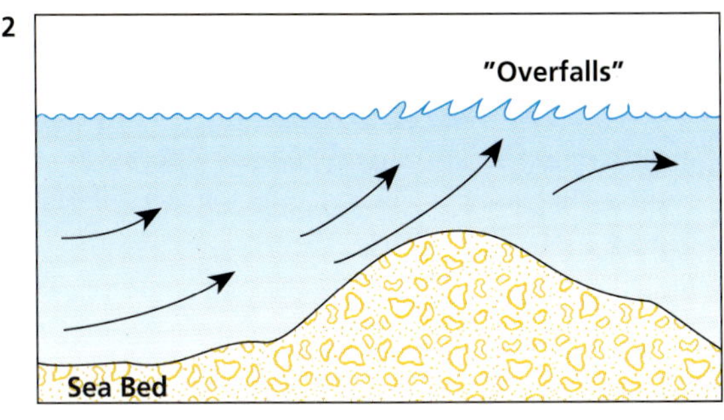

Estimating position

When making any passage at sea an estimate of the vessel's position must be maintained at all times by carefully recording the course steered and the distance run, and by allowing for all those factors which affect that course such as leeway, surface drift, and tidal stream.

To Estimate Your Position (EP)

1 Convert the course steered by compass to True by applying Deviation and Variation as appropriate **A-B** (this is not usually drawn on the chart).

2 Adjust the bearing of the course **A-B** to leeward (downwind) by the amount of leeway suffered to obtain the Water Track True.

3 From the last known position on the chart plot the Water Track and along it mark off the distance run according to the log.
A-C

4 From point **C** plot the set of tidal stream experienced using units of length equal to its rate in knots.
C-D

5 Point **D** is the boat's Estimated Position and a line drawn between it and the last known position **(A)** is the Course Made Good (or Ground Track) and the distance along it is the actual distance covered over the ground.
A-D

This distance, divided by the elapsed time, is the boat's effective speed over the ground.

Plotting the estimated position (EP)

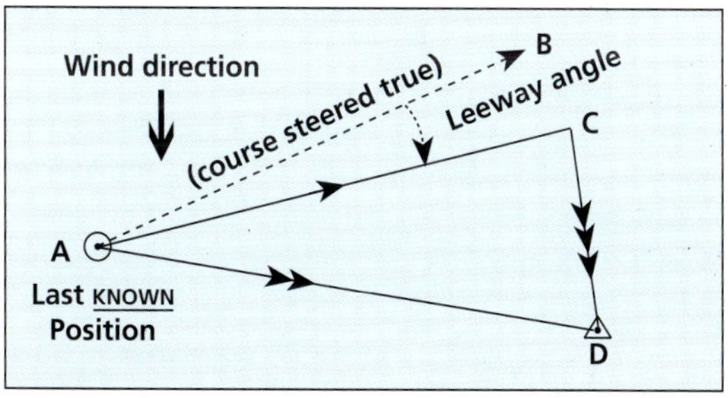

Compass Conversion
applied to course steered

Variation/Deviation **East**
Add the error

Variation/Deviation **West**
Subtract the error

Estimated Leeway suffered
applied to course steered

Wind from **Port** side
Add the angle

Wind from **Starboard** side
Subtract the angle

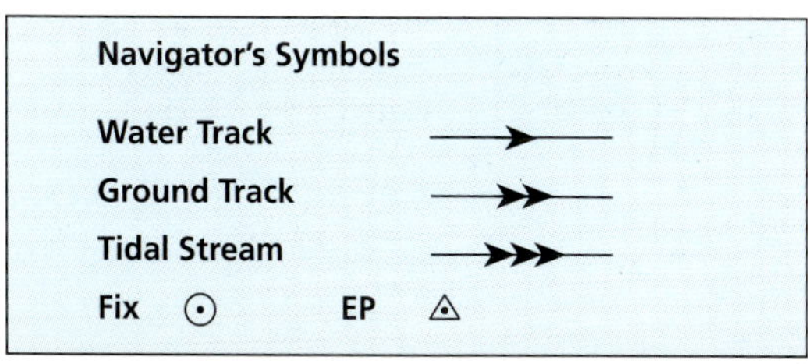

Position fixing

Sadly, the procedure for estimating position is far from perfect, and errors are apt to accumulate in the reckoning which means that the boat's position must periodically be 'fixed' relative to the land if the plot is not to become more and more uncertain as time passes. One method of fixing position when coastal sailing is that of taking visual bearings on charted objects by Hand Bearing Compass.

When the bearing of a known object is drawn onto a chart it is called a Position Line and at some point along it the observer and his vessel must lie *Fig 1*. The intersection of two or more such position lines will mark the position of the observer at the time that the bearings were taken *Fig 2*.

It is important to recognise, however, that due to the motion of small boats, any bearing taken from them by compass is likely to be 'out' by as much as 5° either way and so there is always a sector of uncertainty which must be considered when plotting a position obtained in this way *Fig 3*.

Position lines

1

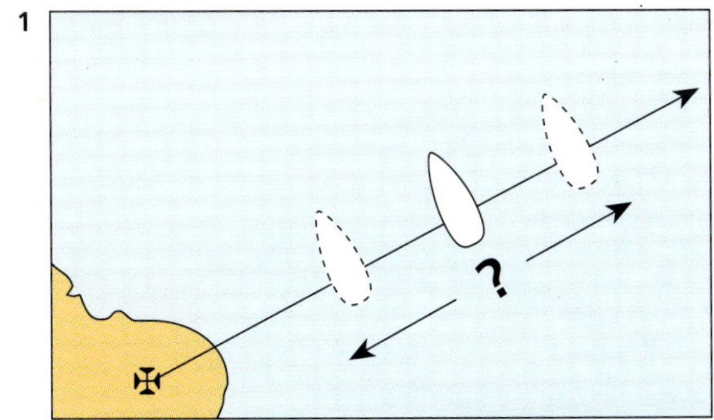

2

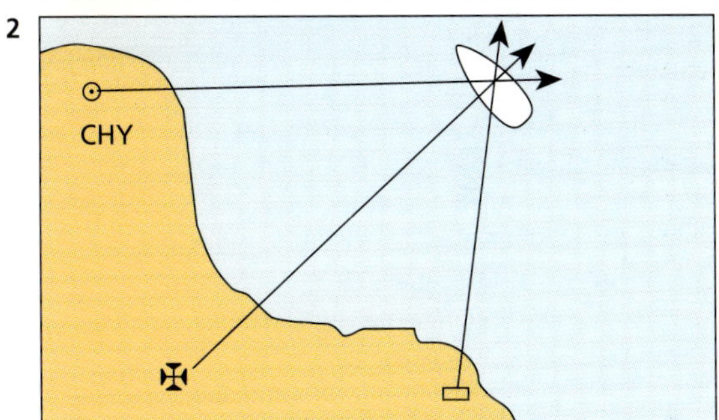

3

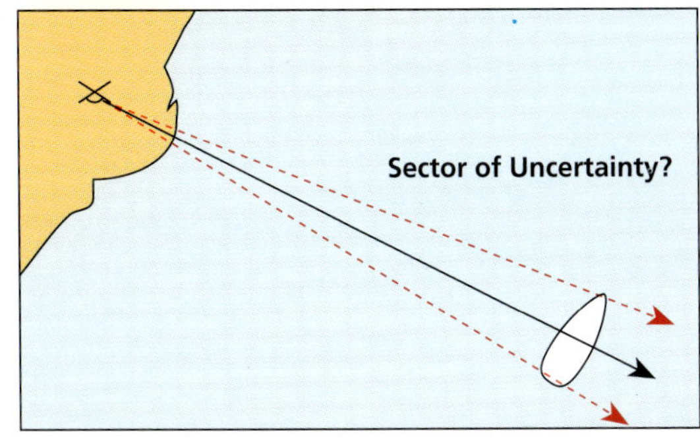

Visual bearings

To fix your position by this means, identify two - preferably three - objects on the coastline that also appear on your chart.

Using a Hand Bearing Compass, take the bearing of each object in turn and make a note of the time and the log reading *Fig 1*.

Convert the Magnetic bearings to True by applying variation as necessary and on the chart draw the appropriate bearing from each object to seaward.

Due to the motion of the boat, none of the bearings are likely to be completely accurate and so the intersection of three position lines will probably result in a 'cocked hat'. The size of this will give an indication of the reliability of the Fix. If it is not too large, it is acceptable, but it should not be assumed that the position lies at the centre of the cocked hat, it may be close, but the wary navigator will always presume it to be situated at a point biased toward the nearest danger along the course being steered *Fig 2*.

The three point fix

1

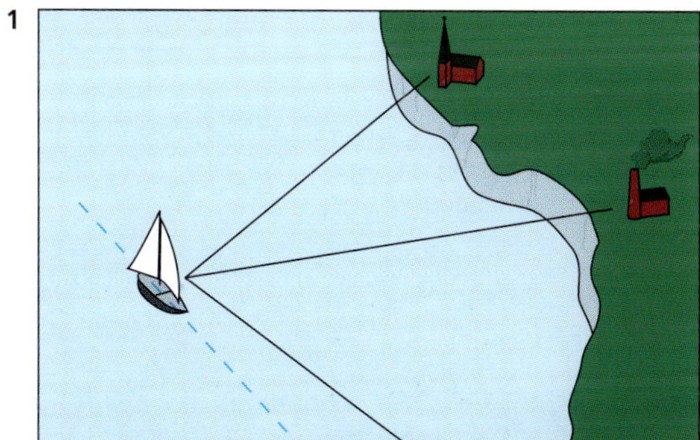

What you see

2

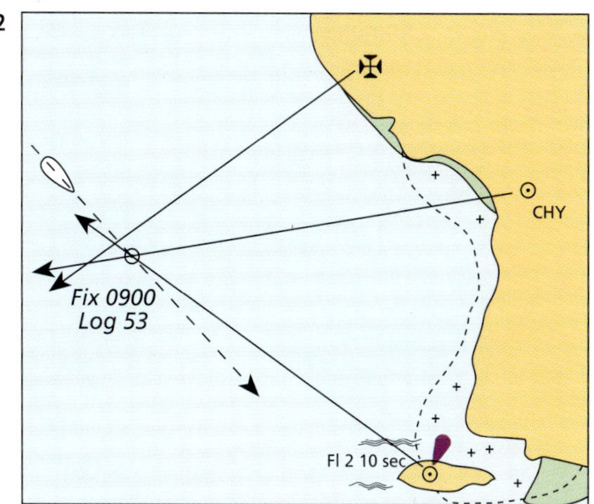

On the Chart

Transits

The simplest of position lines is obtained when it can be seen that two objects that also appear on the chart are in transit (in line with one another). Position lines obtained from transits are very accurate but should only be made with two fixed and well separated objects.

Transits can be found on any chart by lining up towers, spires, and masts etc and, with care, even the prominent edges of land. Transits can be observed without the aid of any instrument other than binoculars perhaps, and all the observer needs to do is to draw a line on the chart that passes through both objects that are in transit to be certain that his vessel lies somewhere along that line *Fig 1*.

It is rare that two transits can be observed simultaneously *Fig 2*, more usually a transit is combined with position lines derived from other sources, i.e. RDF bearings, soundings, or with compass bearings of another fixed object *Fig 3*.

1

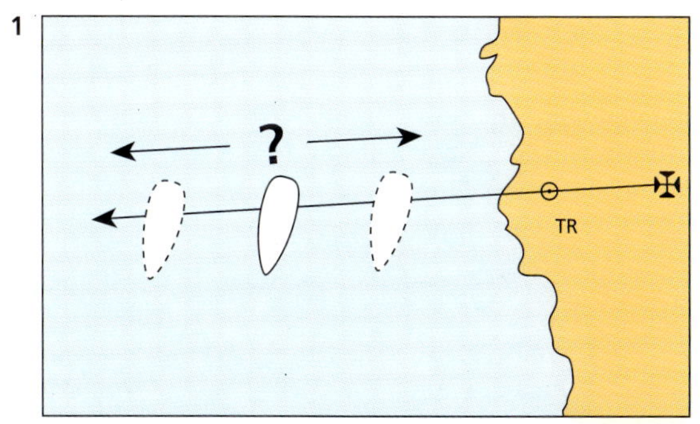

2

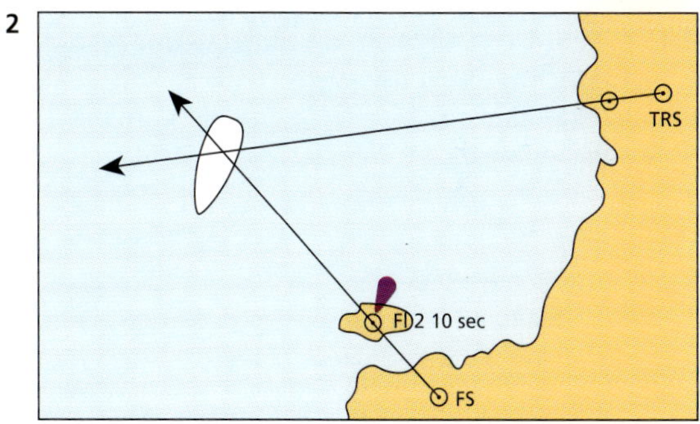

3

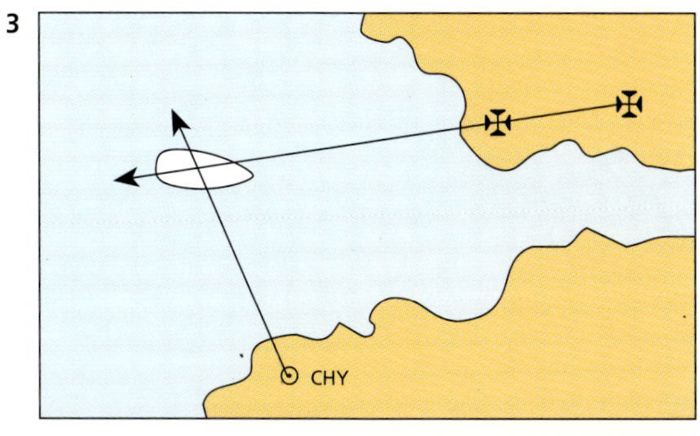

The running fix

Position lines are normally used in combination to 'Fix' position and so the value of a single bearing is not always fully appreciated, however when only one object is visible a procedure known as the Running Fix or Transferred Position Line may be used to establish your approximate position *Fig 1*.

At 0900 the bearing of the lighthouse is taken and the log is read. One hour later, the log is read again and a second bearing on the light is taken.

On the chart, draw both bearings **A** and **B** from the lighthouse *Fig 2*. Then, starting from **any** point on line **A**, work out your EP by plotting your True course since 0900 allowing for leeway and tidal stream. Now draw a line parallel to line **A** so that it passes through your EP and cuts line **B**. The cut on line **B** is your approximate position by 'Running Fix'.

NOTE The position so found should not be regarded as an 'absolute fix' because of possible errors in bearings, log reading, or tidal stream etc.

1

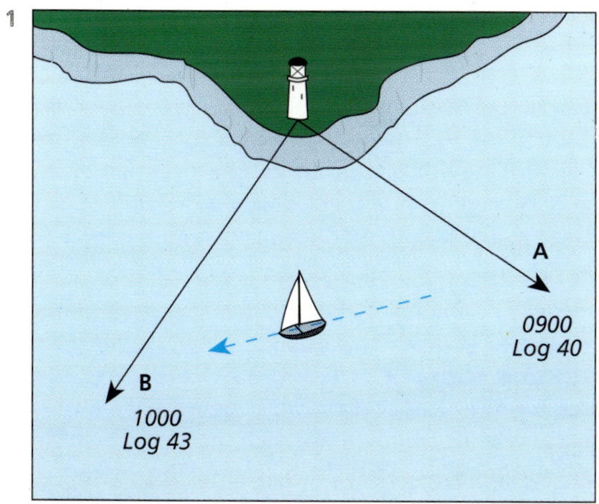

What you see

2

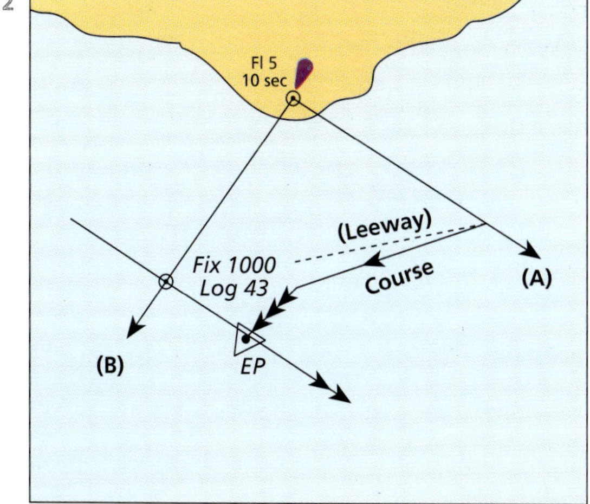

On the chart

Abeam and four point bearing

(a special case for a running fix)

When coastal sailing and the tidal stream is 'more or less' either with you or against you, the abeam and four point bearing is also a useful technique for establishing your approximate position by bearing and distance from a single object as it can be calculated mentally without reference to tables.

When the object bears 'four points' 045° to your vessel's heading note the log reading. Steer a careful course to maintain your heading and then when the object is abeam (090° to the vessel's heading) read the log again. The difference between the log readings is the distance run through the water. Convert this distance run into distance over the ground by adding or subtracting the tidal stream as appropriate and this distance is the same as your distance off when abeam.

NOTE This method should only be attempted where no special dangers lie near the course line as the position thus obtained is only approximate. The method ***does not work at all*** where there is a strong tidal cross set, and/or a lot of leeway.

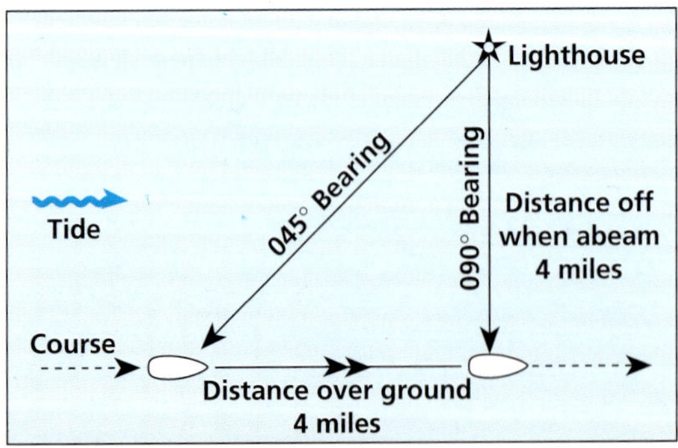

By line of soundings

If the skipper of a yacht steers a steady course across a shelving or uneven sea bed and records a selection of corrected depths *(see page 64)* taken at regular intervals or regular distances by the log, a line of soundings will be obtained from which an approximate position may be found. From the last position on the chart, using the course steered, plot a velocity triangle with the intervals between soundings marked along the water track. From each of these points, draw a line parallel to the tidal stream line to cut the ground track *Fig 1*. Align the edge of a slip of paper with the ground track and onto it jot down the soundings at the ground track intervals. Place the edge of this paper parallel to the ground track to see whether the soundings on the paper coincide with the charted soundings and if they do not, slide the paper around, keeping it parallel to the ground track, until a reasonable match is found *Fig 2*. The position of the last sounding is then assumed to be the yachts approximate position when that sounding was taken.

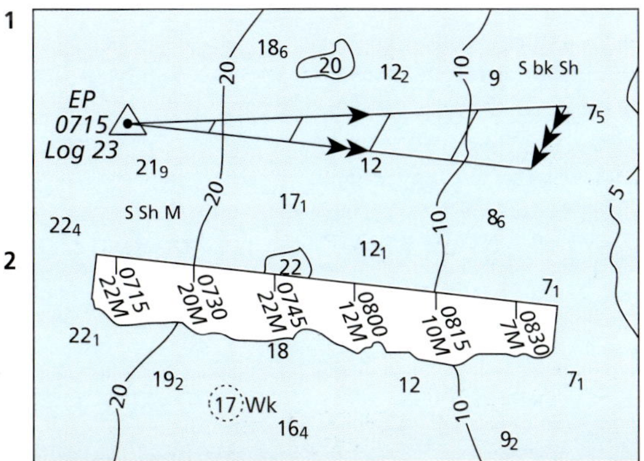

Radio direction finding (RDF)

In spite of the increasing use of hyperbolic navigation aids such as Decca and Loran and the recent advent of the even more sophisticated GPS, for many, the 'good old RDF' is still a useful source of positional information when out of sight of land or in poor visibility. However, it should not be relied upon to the exclusion of normal navigational methods because results achieved depend upon the skill and experience of the user and his understanding of its limitations, i.e. bearings obtained an hour either side of dusk or dawn are unusable and signals which pass overland or along coastlines are not reliable because they are apt to be deflected *Fig 1*.

RDF beacons transmit a morse identification signal followed by a long tone. RDF receivers have an internal ferrite rod aerial to receive these signals and after tuning to the required beacon the receiver is swung until the aerial points end on to the beacon where the signal disappears. This is called the Null and at this point the compass bearing is read *Fig 2*.

It should be noted that as the aerial has two ends it could be pointing either toward OR away from the beacon. If there is any doubt, alter course to seaward and take a series of bearings on the beacon. The change (to left or right) in these bearings will indicate in which direction the beacon lies *Fig 3*.

Coastal refraction

1

Do not take a bearing if the angle to the coast is 15° or less – signals which cross or pass along coastlines at oblique angles may be deflected toward or away from the coast.

15°

Beacon

The Null

2

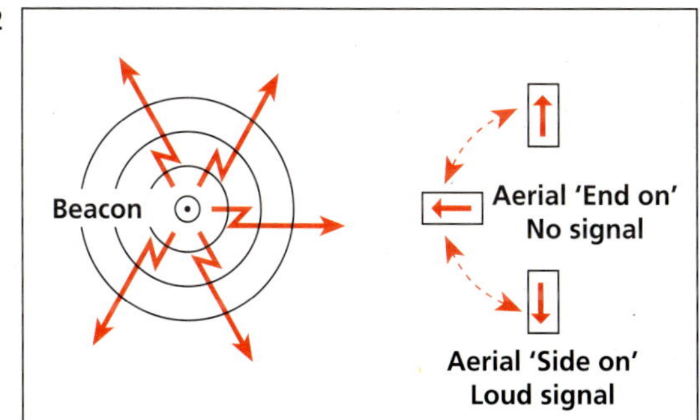

3

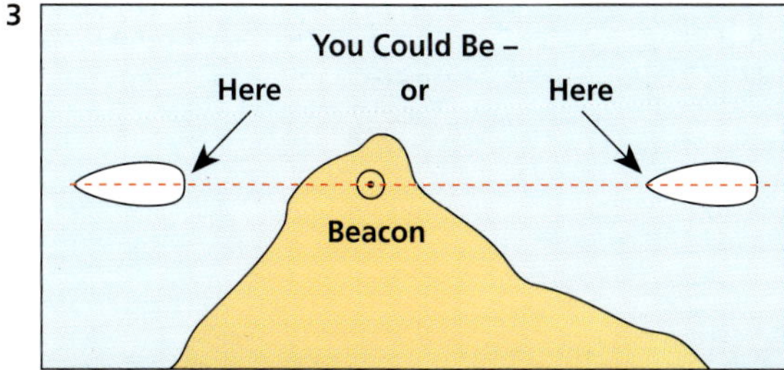

Destination to windward

When your destination lies directly up wind of the boat it becomes necessary to beat towards it by sailing close hauled on alternate tacks, preferably keeping within 10°-15° of the downwind line so as to be well placed to take advantage of any wind shifts as they occur. Set off on the tack which points more directly toward your destination and work up to it with a series of relatively short tacks made between predetermined tack 'limiting lines' making due allowance for leeway and tidal stream in the usual way. Alternatively, if your objective is visible you can tack each time the appropriate bearing to either side of the direct line of approach is reached *Fig 1*.

1

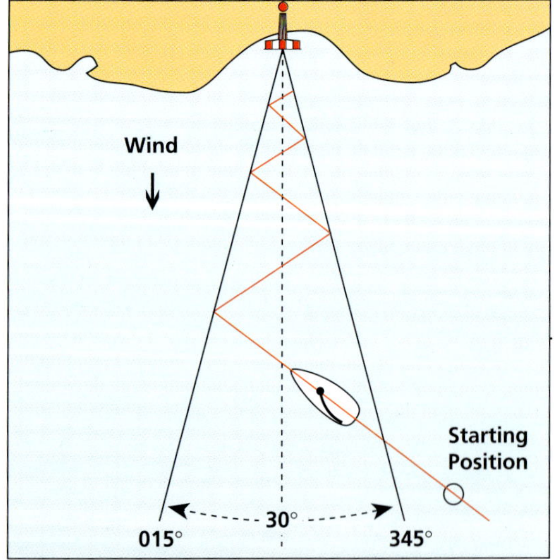

Lee bowing the tide

If the tidal stream is expected to slacken or reverse direction, there is an advantage to be gained from holding the tack which puts the tide on the lee bow and letting it push the boat to windward. The freeing wind shift induced by the tide will also allow the boat to point higher on this tack, helping to get you towards your destination more quickly.

If the tidal stream is constant, however, there is no advantage to 'lee bowing' as you will lose whatever you have gained when you go onto the opposite tack *Fig 2*.

2

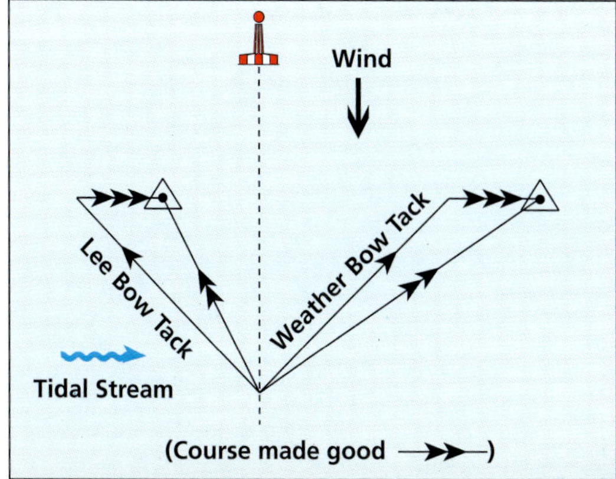

Laying the windward mark

When nearing your destination, if wind and tide are going to remain unchanged, it is possible to work out just when to make your final tack to lay the buoy *Fig 3*.

3

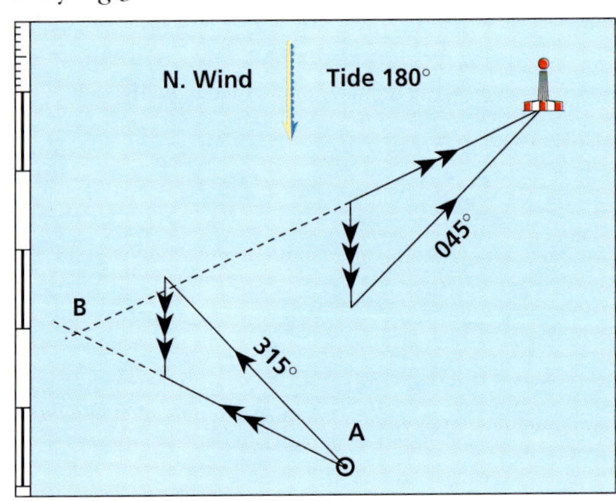

You are at point A on starboard tack, heading 315° at 4kt and your boat will tack through 90°. Tidal stream rate is 1·5kt. First, find out what the ground track will be from **A** and extend it, then work out what the ground track will be as you head for the buoy on port tack. To do this, draw the water track ***backwards*** from the buoy and along it mark off 4 miles for boat speed. Plot 1·5 miles of tidal stream ***reversed*** and from the end of this draw a line to the buoy to obtain the ground track. Extend this line to intersect the ground track from **A** and where they cross at **B** is the place to tack. The length of the ground track shows that the boat speed over the ground is about 3·1kt and since the distance to **B** from position **A** is almost 4·5 miles, you will reach position **B** in about 87 minutes.

Estimated time of arrival (ETA)

To calculate ***when*** you will get there, you must know the distance to your destination, the boat's speed through the water, and what the tide is doing. i.e.

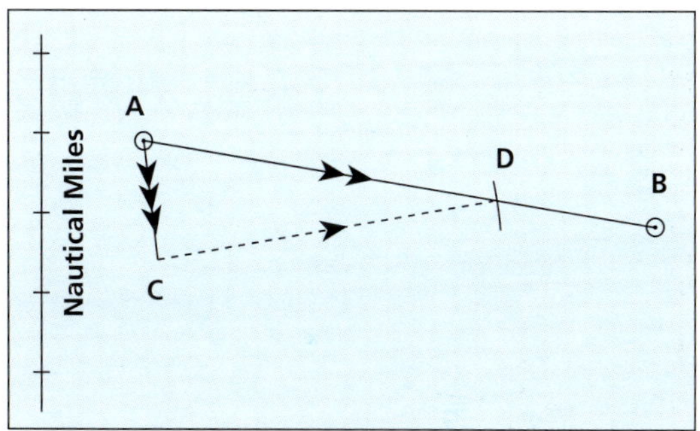

A **The starting position**

B **The destination**

A-B **The distance to go (6·9m)**

A-C **Tidal stream vector (1·5kt)**

From **C** with dividers set at a distance equal to the boat's speed through the water, (4·5kt) swing an arc to cut line A-B at point **D**.

A-D is the speed (and distance) made good, (4·8kt) therefore **A-B x 60 ÷ A-D** is equal to the time in minutes that it will take to sail from **A** to **B** and if this time is added to your time of departure from position A then this will be your ETA at your destination.

$$\frac{\textbf{A-B}}{\textbf{A-D}} \times 60 = 86{\cdot}25 \text{ mins}$$

Say $1\frac{1}{2}$ hrs approx.

'Tides' are the vertical rise and fall of the sea's surface caused by the gravitational 'pull' of the Sun and Moon. When the Sun and Moon are in line with the Earth, their combined influence creates very high and very low waters known as **Spring** Tides, but when the Sun and Moon are at right angles to the Earth, their effect is much less and so more moderate tides known as **Neap** Tides occur, *Fig 1.*

1

Sun
NP
SP
Earth
SP
NP

Spring Tides occur about every 14 days at the time of Full and New Moons. Neap Tides occur during the alternate weeks when the Moon is in its First or Third Quarter, *Fig 2.*

2

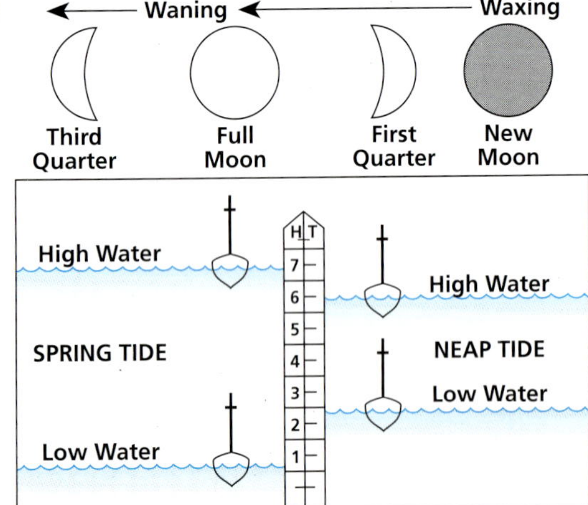

Tidal stream

A tidal stream is the horizontal movement of water caused by the rise and fall of the tide. Spring Tides create strong tidal streams, Neap Tides relatively weaker ones. The direction and strength of tidal stream is given on most charts and is related to the time of high water and the range of tide at a specific port. Tidal Atlases also provide information about tidal streams and include graphs for computing the rate of streams at times between Springs or Neaps, *(see pages 18 and 20)*. Times and heights of high and low water are given in annual Tide Tables and Nautical Almanacs.

The range of the tide is the vertical difference in height between successive high and low waters.

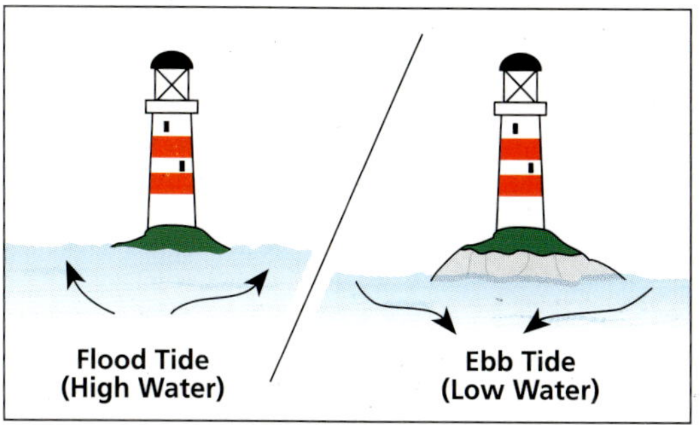

The 'Interval' between successive high waters around the British Isles is approximately 12hr 25min.

Definitions of tidal levels and data

The level of the sea is constantly changing as the tide rises and falls and so, on a chart, depths of water and drying heights are measured from a common state of the tide known as the Lowest Astronomical Tide (LAT). This is the lowest level to which the tide is expected to fall due to any combination of astronomical conditions and is the CHART DATUM.

Chart Datum: The level to which Soundings and Drying Heights are referred on the chart and the level above which Height of Tide is measured.

Charted Sounding: The depth to the sea bed below the level of Chart Datum. Shown on the chart by figures in metres and tenths of metres, i.e. 6_5.

Drying Height: The height above Chart Datum of a feature that is periodically covered and uncovered by the tide shown on the chart by ***underlined*** figures in metres and tenths of metres, i.e. $\underline{2}_4$.

Height of Tide: The vertical distance between Chart Datum and the sea level at any given time.

Mean High Water Springs (MHWS)
Mean Low Water Springs (MLWS)

The average height of high and low water at Spring Tides.

> MHWS is the level from which the charted heights of terrestrial objects are measured.

Mean High Water Neaps (MHWN)
Mean Low Water Neaps (MLWN)

The average height of high and low water at Neap Tides.

Tidal heights and chart datum

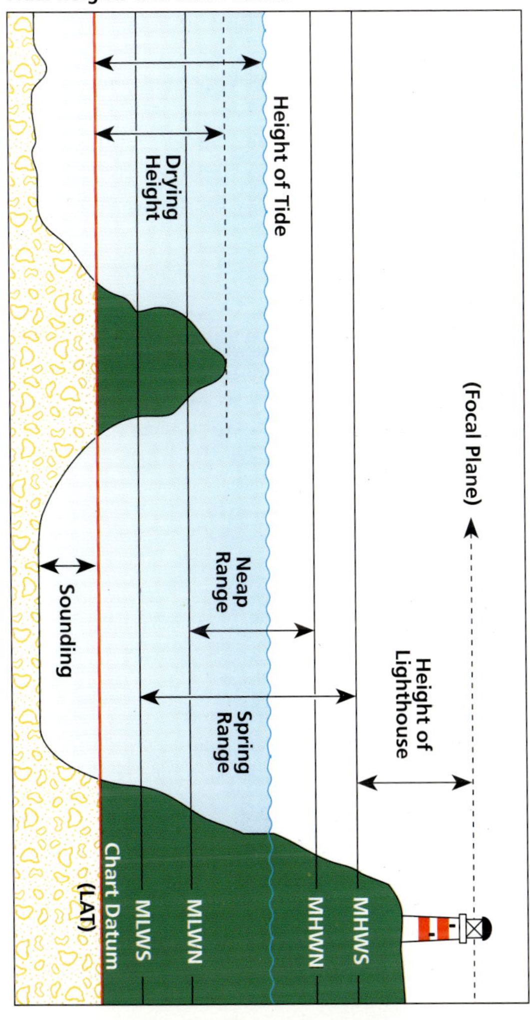

Standard Ports

In the almanac each Standard Port is given its own Tide Table and Tidal Curves. The time and height of high and low water is read directly from the table and the curves are used to find the height of tide at any other time between high and low water i.e.

On 1st May at Walton-on-the-Naze

a What will the height of tide be at 1100 GMT? *and*

b At what time will the tide reach a height of 1·75m?

First, mark up the graph with the WALTON high and low water times and heights and join the heights with a line as shown. Now compare the predicted range of tide with the mean ranges at Springs and Neaps and decide which curve to use or whether to interpolate between them *(see page 54 for interpolation between curves)*.

To answer a

Enter the graph at the required time - 1100 and proceed as shown by the **RED** line to find the height of tide at this time - 2·9m approx.

To answer b

Enter the graph at the height required - 1·75m and proceed as shown by the **BLUE** line to find the time at which this height will occur, 0920 GMT approx.

The height found by graph when added to the depth shown on the chart is the actual depth at that place.

A drying height shown on the chart when subtracted from the height found by graph will be the depth (if any) at that place.

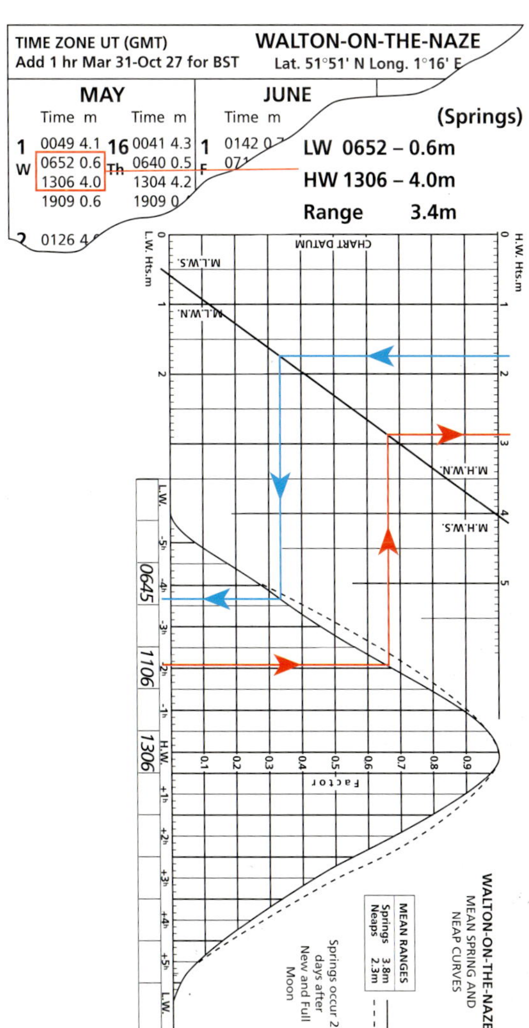

TIME ZONE UT (GMT)
Add 1 hr Mar 31-Oct 27 for BST
WALTON-ON-THE-NAZE
Lat. 51°51' N Long. 1°16' E
MAY
JUNE
Time m
1 W 0049 4.1
0652 0.6
1306 4.0
1909 0.6
16 Th 0041 4.3
0640 0.5
1304 4.2
1909 0
1 F 0142 0
2 0126 4
(Springs)
LW 0652 – 0.6m
HW 1306 – 4.0m
Range 3.4m
H.W. Hts.m
L.W. Hts.m
CHART DATUM
M.L.W.S.
M.L.W.N.
M.H.W.N.
M.H.W.S.
Factor
0645
1106
1306
L.W.
H.W.
WALTON-ON-THE-NAZE
MEAN SPRING AND NEAP CURVES
MEAN RANGES
Springs 3.8m
Neaps 2.3m
Springs occur 2 days after New and Full Moon

Interpolation between Spring and Neap curves

When using tidal curves and the range of tide for the required day lies somewhere between the mean Spring and Neap ranges, 'REED'S' method of interpolation between the curves will provide a much more accurate answer than the more usual 'guesstimate'.

The procedure is similar to that detailed on page 52 except that the answers are extracted from ***both*** curves and then transferred to the boxes below to obtain an exact interpolation.

To find the predicted height of tide at Ullapool at 0700 on a given day

Predicted height of High Water 5.0m Time 1045

Predicted height of Low Water 1.2m

Range 3.8m *(between Spring and Neap)*

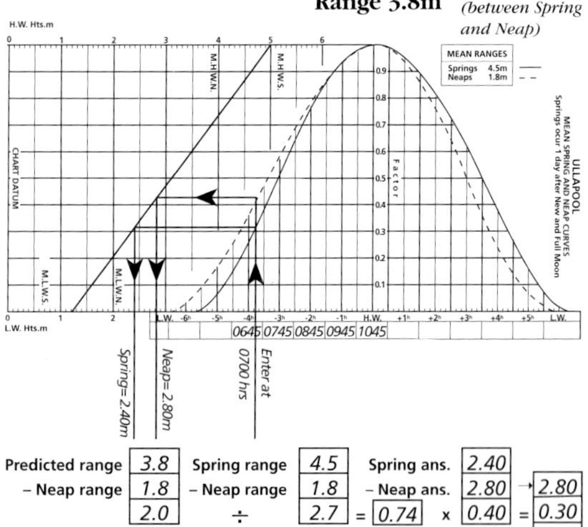

Predicted range	3.8	Spring range	4.5		Spring ans.	2.40		
– Neap range	1.8	– Neap range	1.8		– Neap ans.	2.80	→	2.80
	2.0	÷	2.7	= 0.74	x	0.40	=	0.30
								2.50

Note that the final answer must lie between the Spring and Neap answers.

The **time** at which the tide will reach a **given height** is found in much the same way and the procedure for this calculation is illustrated below.

To find the time at which the tide will reach 2.5m at Ullapool

Predicted height of High Water 5.0m Time 1045

Predicted height of Low Water 1.2m

Range 3.8m *(between Spring and Neap)*

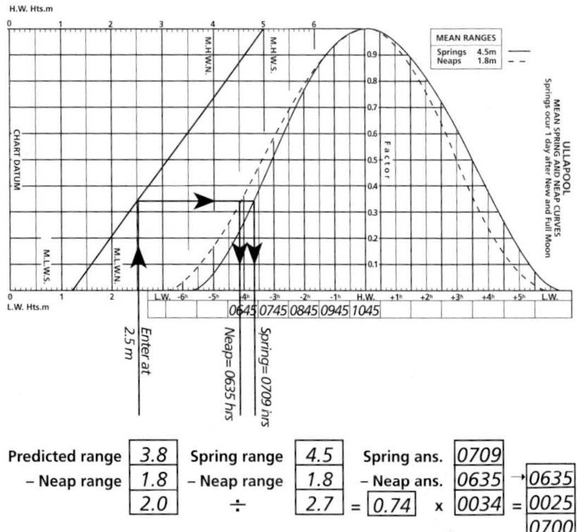

Note that the final answer must lie between the Spring and Neap answers.

Secondary ports - tidal differences

Tidal predictions are published in full for selected places called Standard Ports, but tidal data for smaller Secondary Ports must be found by applying local corrections - tabulated in the almanac as 'differences' - to the standard port times and heights.

For example:

STANDARD PORT: WALTON - ON - THE - NAZE							
TIMES				HEIGHTS (Metres)			
HW		LW		MHWS	MHWN	MLWN	MLWS
0000 AND 1200	0600 AND 1800	0500 AND 1700	1100 AND 2300	4.2	3.4	1.1	0.4
DIFFERENCES – BRADWELL							
+0035	+0023	+0047	+0004	+1.1	+0.8	+0.2	+0.1

Time differences

The table is saying that if HW at Walton occurs at either 0000 or 1200 then HW at Bradwell will be 35 minutes later. Alternatively if HW Walton is either 0600 or 1800 then it will occur 23 minutes later at Bradwell.

Similarly if LW occurs at Walton at either 0500 or 1700, LW at Bradwell will be 47 minutes later, but only 4 minutes later if LW Walton is either 1100 or 2300.

Height differences

These are applied in much the same way as time differences, and in this instance the table says that when the height of High Water at Walton is either 4·2 or 3·4m it will be 1·1 or 0·8m higher respectively at Bradwell and when Low Water at Walton is either 1.1 or 0.4m, then, at Bradwell, it will be 0.2 or 0.1m higher respectively.

When the tidal predictions for the day do not coincide exactly with the times and heights specified in the table of differences, interpolation is necessary between the differences to be applied for that port. This can usually be carried out quite satisfactorily 'by eye' but a simple free hand graph is more accurate if the magnitude of the differences varies greatly, *see page 59*.

Interpolation - tidal differences

Example:

On a chosen day HW Walton is 1405 3·8m. It can be seen that 1405 falls between the reference times of 1200 and 1800 on the table of differences *(see page 56)*, therefore the exact difference which has to be applied lies proportionally between +35 to +23mins (about +30min by eye).

To be more accurate than this, draw a graph as shown with the Walton reference times 1200 to 1800 along one side and their corresponding differences for Bradwell +35 to +23min along the opposite side (see note page 59). Close the triangle by drawing a line A-B between the last units on upper and lower lines.

Enter the graph with HW Walton 1405 and draw a line ***parallel to line A-B*** to cut the lower line where the difference to be applied can now be read off (+31min).

The height of HW at Walton, 3·8, falls between 4·2 and 3·4m on the table of differences which means that the difference to apply lies between 1·1 and 0·8m. The precise difference could be found by constructing another graph with reference heights along one side and the corresponding differences along the other but in this instance as the range of difference is so small (0.3m) interpolation by eye should be quite adequate.

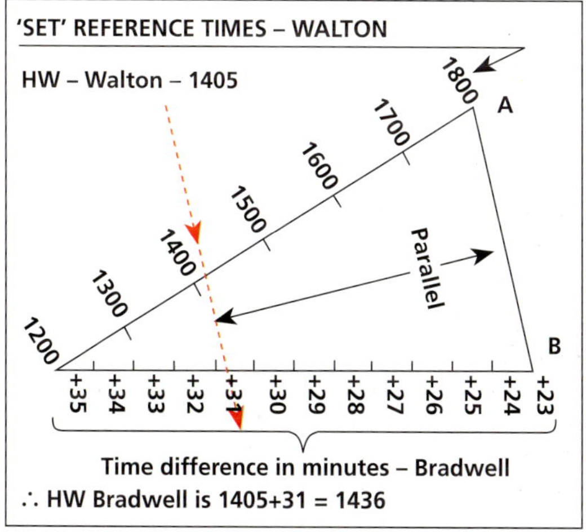

NOTE The triangle may be drawn to ***any*** appropriate size and ***any*** suitable scale may be used, but it is ***essential*** to keep the reference times and their corresponding differences in the correct relationship.

Secondary ports - Intermediate heights

The time and height of high and low water at a Secondary Port is obtained by applying the differences tabulated in the almanac to the Standard Port's tidal predictions.

Secondary Ports do not usually have their own Tidal Curves so when the height of tide at any time between that of high and low water at a Secondary Port is required the curve belonging to the Standard Port is used after first marking it up with the corrected tidal information (both times and heights) for the Secondary Port as shown below.

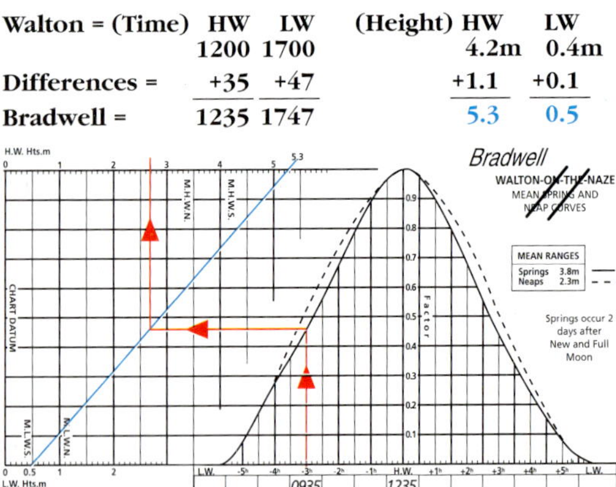

	(Time) HW	LW	(Height) HW	LW
Walton =	1200	1700	4.2m	0.4m
Differences =	+35	+47	+1.1	+0.1
Bradwell =	1235	1747	5.3	0.5

When the Secondary Port tidal data has been entered onto the Standard Port graph, heights of tide at intermediate time e.g. 0935 at the Secondary Port can quickly be found by following the procedure detailed on page 52.

Height of tide by rule of twelfths

This rule gives a rough guide to the change of depth by assuming that the tidal cycle is symmetrical and that the duration of rise or fall is approximately six hours. Unfortunately the tide does not rise or fall evenly for each hour between high and low water and it also varies from place to place. For this reason all calculations by this method should be regarded as very approximate and should be used with great caution and with a generous margin for error.

The Rule States that the Rate of Rise or Fall is:

During the	1st Hour	1/12	of the Range.
"	2nd Hour	2/12	"
"	3rd Hour	3/12	"
"	4th Hour	3/12	"
"	5th Hour	2/12	"
"	6th Hour	1/12	"

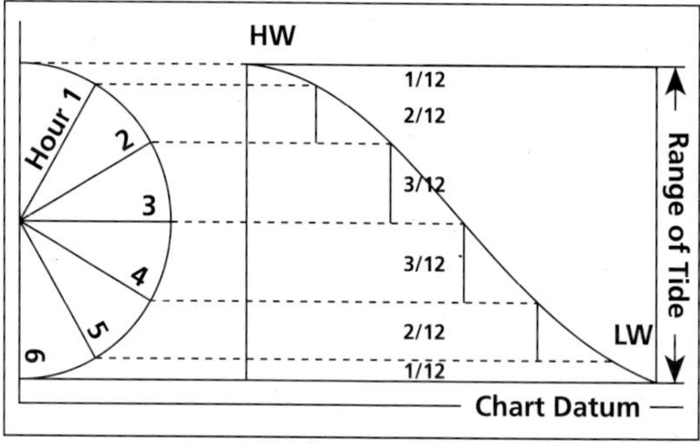

Anomalies–South coast

Very complicated tides occur in the region between Swanage and Selsey where times of low water are more easily defined than times of high water. For this reason special tidal curves with times relative to **low water** have been produced for Secondary Ports in this area. In all other respects the procedure for finding heights of tide at intermediate times with these curves is identical to that used for normal Secondary Ports except that as the tides at some of these places cannot be defined properly by two curves, a third 'critical' curve has been introduced for the range of tide at the Standard Port - Portsmouth - and any interpolation necessary should take place between this third curve and either the Spring or Neap curve as appropriate i.e.

Find height of tide at Lymington at 2130 BST when at the Standard Port tidal predictions are:-

LW 1905 BST - 1·1m
HW 0204 BST - 4·5m

1 Find the tidal data for Lymington by applying the differences to Portsmouth in the usual way.

2 Mark the corrected time and heights found onto the Lymington graph and join the heights with a line in the normal way.

3 Enter the graph at the time required - 2130 - and proceed as shown by the red line to obtain the height of tide at this time.

In this example the range of tide at Portsmouth is very close to that of the critical curve so any interpolation that is necessary should be between the critical curve and the Spring curve.

South Coast - Lymington and Yarmouth

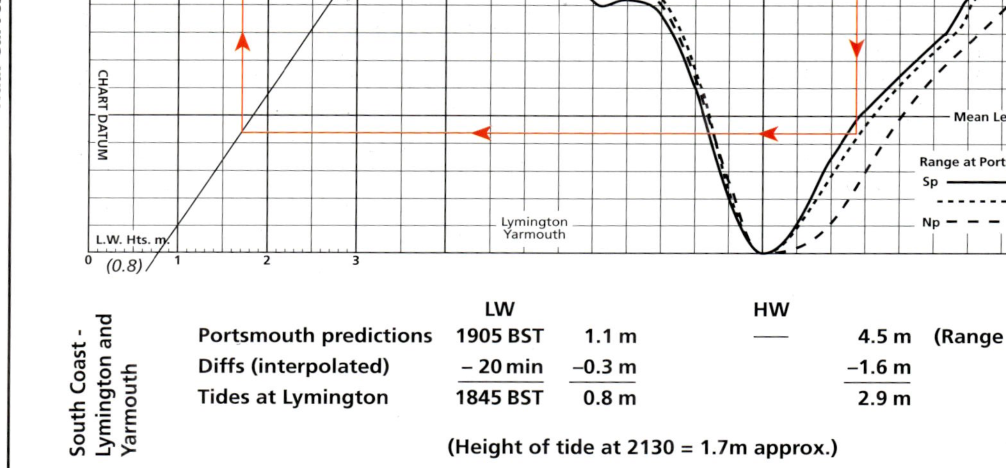

	LW		HW		
Portsmouth predictions	1905 BST	1.1 m	—	4.5 m	(Range 3.4m)
Diffs (interpolated)	– 20 min	–0.3 m		–1.6 m	
Tides at Lymington	1845 BST	0.8 m		2.9 m	

(Height of tide at 2130 = 1.7m approx.)

When a sounding is taken in tidal waters it cannot be related to the depths which are shown on the chart until the height of tide prevailing at that time and place has been established and subtracted from the sounding.

This procedure is called 'reduction to soundings' and forms an important part of several tidal calculations including the confirmation of an estimated position or to assist in Pilotage when 'running a line of soundings'. *(See page 41).*

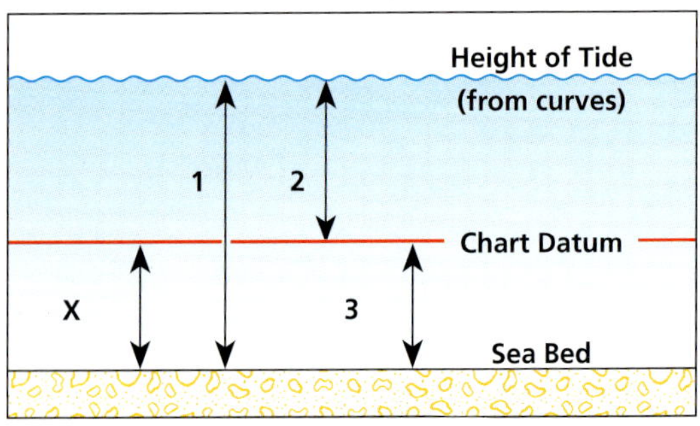

X	Charted sounding
1	Sounding taken
2	Minus height of tide
3	Is the reduced sounding

3 and X should more or less agree if your EP is correct.

Height of tide reduced to soundings

Using handline and lead

1. Depth by handline and lead	
2. minus height of tide	
3. is – the reduced sounding	

A favourable comparison between the reduced sounding obtained and the charted sounding for your estimated position will help to confirm your EP.

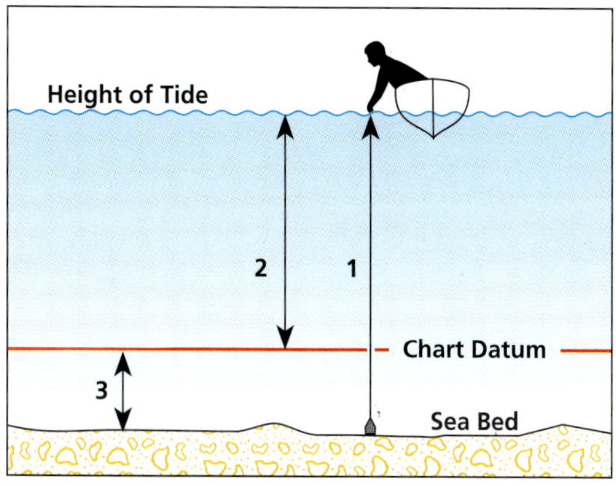

Height of tide reduced to soundings

Using echo sounder calibrated to read from the vessel's waterline

1. Echo sounder reading	
2. minus height of tide	
3. is – the reduced sounding	

Compare the reduced sounding obtained to the charted sounding at your EP to confirm the position.

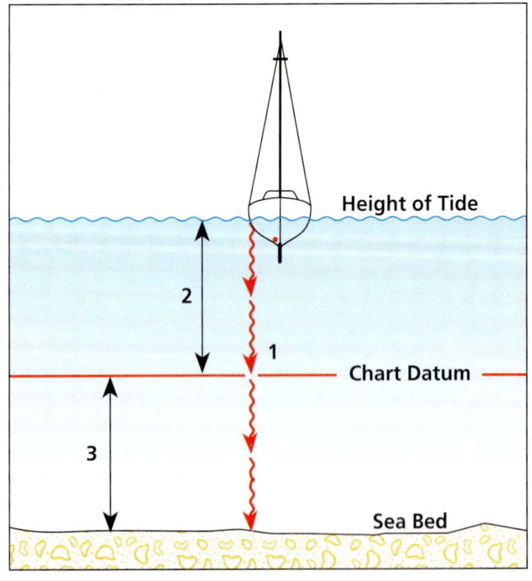

Height of tide reduced to soundings

Using uncalibrated echo sounder

1. Echo sounder reading	
2. plus distance transducer to waterline	
3. is – the actual depth	
4. minus height of tide	
5. is – the reduced sounding	

Compare the reduced sounding obtained to the charted sounding at your EP to confirm the position.

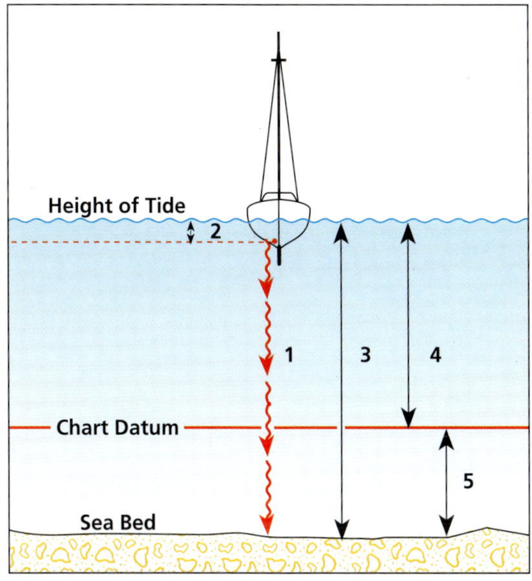

Height of tide reduced to soundings

Using echo sounder calibrated to read from below the keel

1. Echo sounder reading	
2. plus draught of vessel	
3. is – the actual depth	
4. minus height of tide	
5. is – reduced sounding	

Compare the reduced sounding obtained to the charted sounding at your EP to confirm the position.

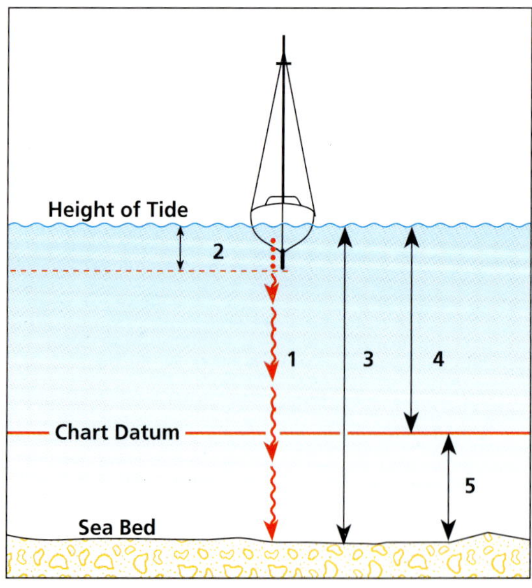

Finding depth by echo sounder

To avoid going aground at low tide

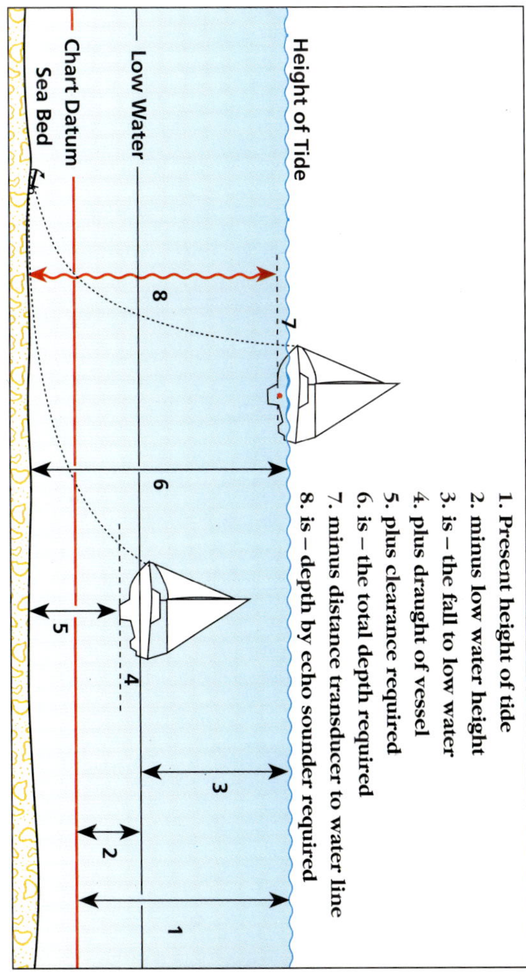
1. Present height of tide
2. minus low water height
3. is – the fall to low water
4. plus draught of vessel
5. plus clearance required
6. is – the total depth required
7. minus distance transducer to water line
8. is – depth by echo sounder required
Height of Tide
Low Water
Chart Datum
Sea Bed
1
2
3
4
5
6
7
8

Will there be enough water at low tide?

A quick and easy way of finding the depth in which to anchor without calculation.

Preparation

1 Find the times and heights of high and low water for the area you are in and plot the heights on your nearest Standard Port tidal curve as line A.

2 Mark on the low water line the minimum depth at which you want to be afloat - (draught plus safety margin) - and from this point draw a line ***parallel*** to line A.

From now on line A is disregarded and anytime you want to anchor the required depth can be read off quickly by reference to line B.

Example:- If HW at Walton is 3·5m at 1200 and LW is 0·8m at 1800, plot this on the curve as line A.

Now mark your minimum anchoring depth - say 2m - on the low water line and from it draw line B ***parallel*** to line A.

When you want to anchor, just check the time and draw a line up to the appropriate curve, across to line B then up or down to find the safest minimum depth to drop anchor.

In this instance - at 0920 - just circle round until your echo sounder reads 3·6m or more.

Predictions	HW 1200	3.5 Range 2.7
	LW 1800	0.8

Time required – 0920 **Min depth required – 2m**

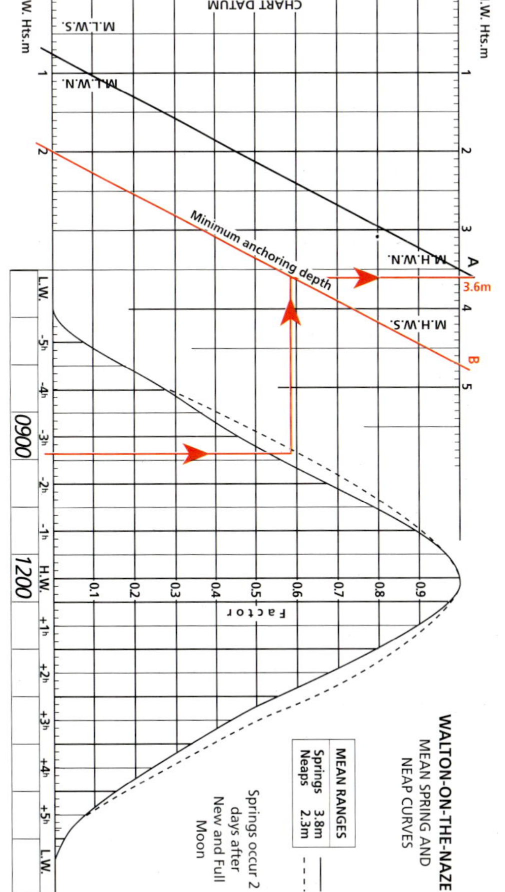

To find clearance at low water

Using hand line and lead

1. Depth by handline	
2. minus present height of tide	
3. is – depth below Chart Datum	
4. plus height of Low Water	
5. is – depth at Low Water	
6. minus draught of vessel	
7. is – clearance at Low Water	

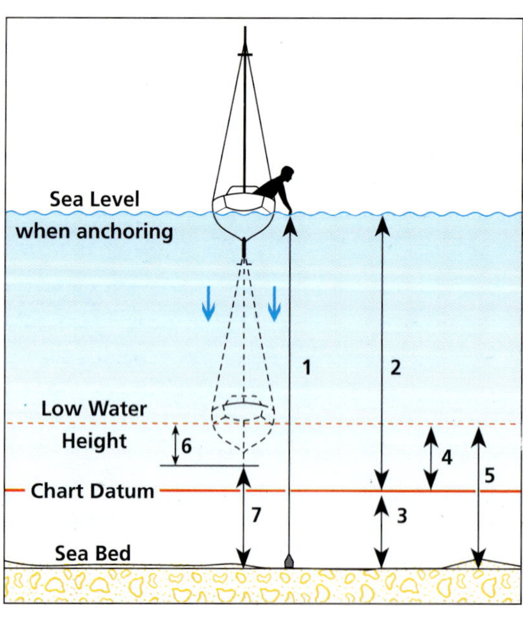

To find clearance at low water

Using echo sounder

1. Echo sounder reading	
2. plus distance – transducer to waterline	
3. is – true depth of water	
4. minus present height of tide	
5. is – depth below Chart Datum	
6. plus height of next Low Water	
7. is – depth at Low Water	
8. minus draught of vessel	
9. will be – clearance at Low Water	

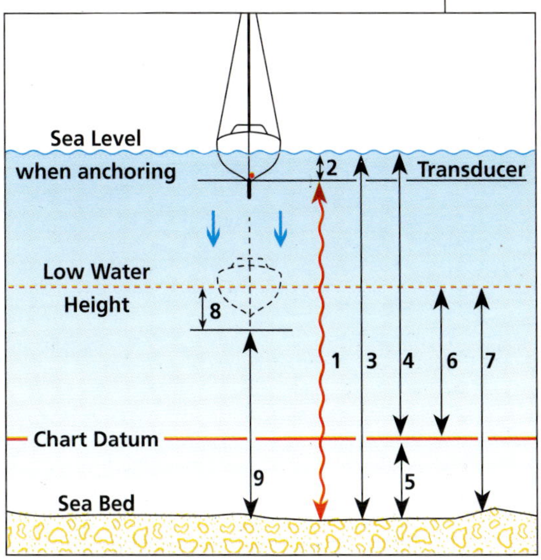

What is the depth beneath my keel?

1. Present height of tide	
2. plus charted sounding	
3. is – total depth of water	
4. minus draught of vessel	
5. is – depth below the keel	

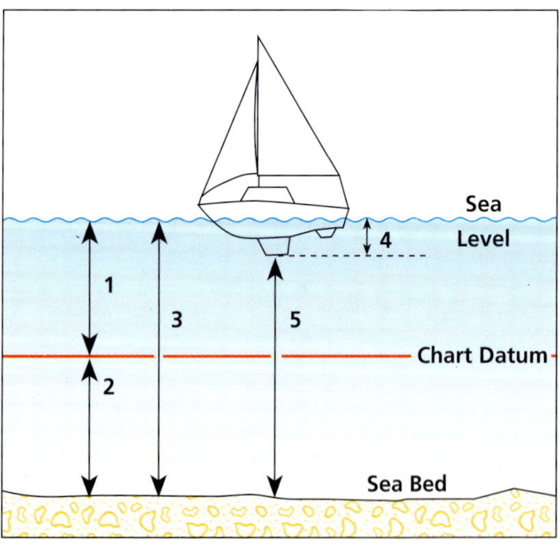

Use tidal curve to calculate the present height of tide.

Height of tide required to clear a bank or bar

1. Draught of the vessel	
2. plus clearance required	
3. is – total depth required	
4. minus charted sounding	
5. is – height of tide required	

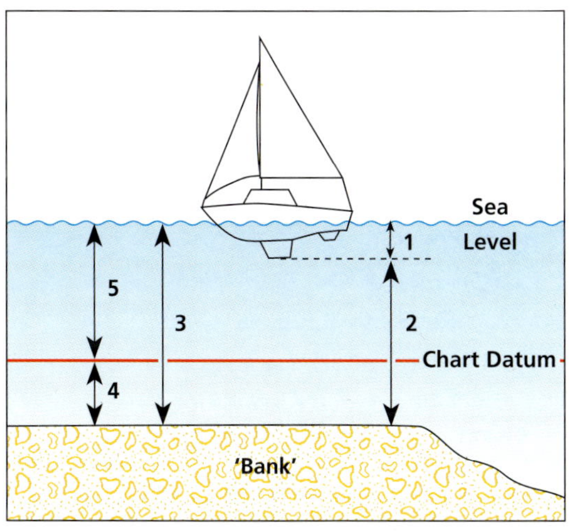

Use tidal curve to find time at which height required will occur.

Height of tide

Required to clear a charted drying height

1. Draught of vessel	
2. plus clearance required	
3. plus charted drying height	
4. is – height of tide required	

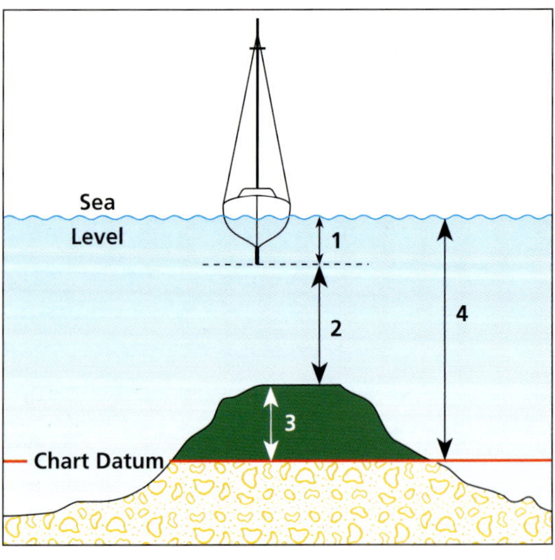

Use tidal curve to find the time at which the required height will occur.

Will my vessel clear a charted drying height?

1. Present height of tide	
2. minus drying height	
3. is – actual depth of water	
4. minus draught of vessel	
5. is – clearance below the keel	

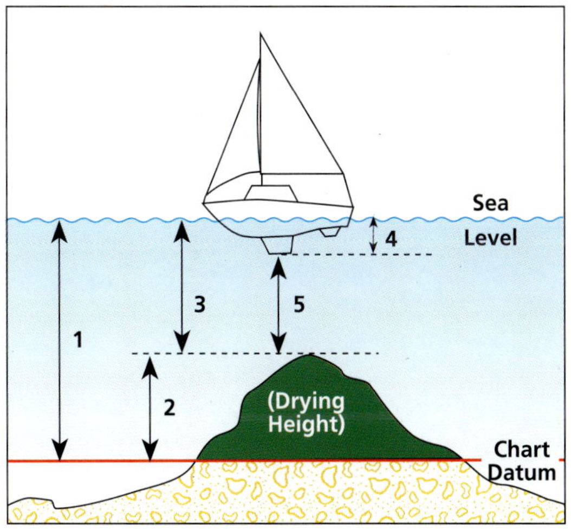

On a Falling Tide

Use tidal curve to find the latest time to cross in safety.

On a Rising Tide

Use tidal curve to find the time at which the required height will occur.

On nautical charts, symbols and abbreviations are used to convey a mass of navigational information to the mariner. Each symbol has only one meaning, but it is vital that these 'coded messages' are correctly interpreted as many of them warn of specific dangers to navigation. i.e.

	Overfalls, tide rips, races
	Eddies
Obstn Obstn	*Obstruction or danger, exact nature not specified or determined, depth unknown*
4_6 Obstn	*Obstruction, depth known*
4_6 Obstn	*Obstruction which has been swept by wire to the depth shown*
5_8 19 18 Br	*Breakers*
(3·1) (1·7) (4·1)	*Rock which does not cover, height above High Water*
(1_6) 5 (1_6) (5_8)	*Rock which covers and uncovers, height above Chart Datum*
5 0	*Rock awash at the level of Chart Datum*
5 0	*Underwater rock, depth unknown, considered dangerous to surface navigation*
Wk	*Wreck showing any part of hull or superstructure at the level of Chart Datum*
	Wreck, depth unknown, which is considered dangerous to surface navigation
Mast (1·2) Masts Funnel Mast(1_2)	*Wreck of which the mast(s) only are visible at Chart Datum*

A complete list of symbols and abbreviations is provided in Admiralty publication, Chart 5011.

The height of all charted terrestrial features other than drying heights are measured from the level of MHWS tides.

If the height of MHWS above Chart Datum is known it is possible to find the actual height of the feature above sea level by adding its charted height to the level of MHWS at that place and then subtracting the height of tide at the time from the total *Fig 1*.

When the height of the feature has thus been established a 'Distance Off' can be calculated in daytime by vertical sextant angle, *see page 82* or at night by 'Rising or Dipping' of the light, *see page 88*.

1

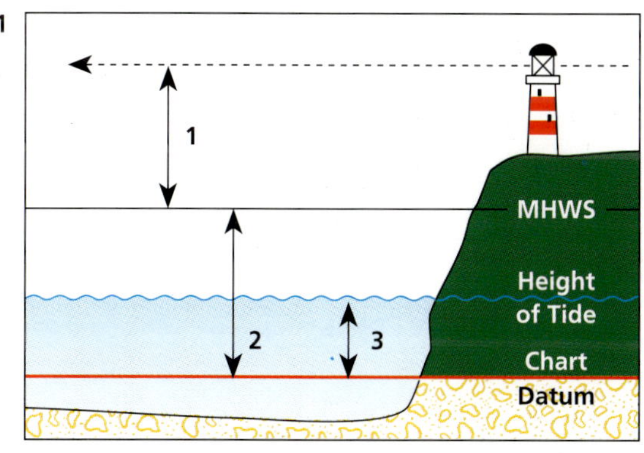

1. Charted height of light	**20m**
2. plus height of MHWS	**6m**
is – the height above Chart Datum	**26m**
3. minus the height of tide	**2**
is – the height above sea level	**24m**

Index error

When coastal sailing, the sextant can be used to fix the boat's position by means of either vertical or horizontal angles of charted objects such as lighthouses etc. Before using it for this purpose the sextant should be adjusted according to the maker's instructions. Any residual error left in the instrument after this is known as 'index error' and its value must be applied as a correction to all future sextant readings.

To find the Index Error

1. Clamp index bar and micrometer drum at zero.
2. Hold the sextant vertically and sight a clear, distant horizon turning the drum until the true and reflected horizons form a single unbroken line.
3. The sextant reading indicates the index error.
4. If the reading is on the 'plus' side of zero it must be subtracted as a correction.
5. If the reading is on the negative side of zero it must be added.

Distance off by vertical sextant angle

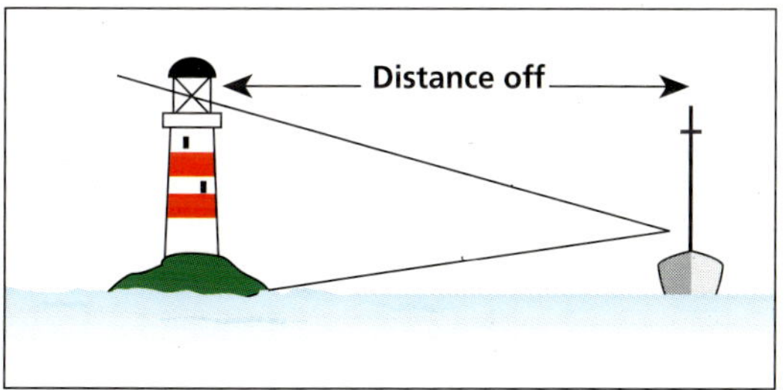

*Vertical angle taken between the base of the Lighthouse and **Focal Plane** of the light - **not** the top of the Lighthouse.*

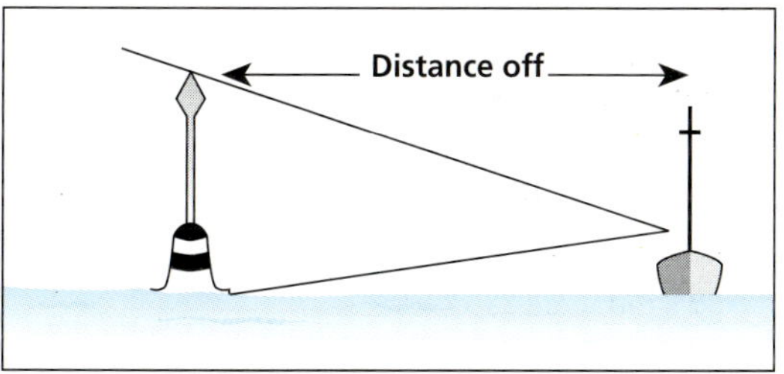

*Vertical angle taken between the base of the object and its **peak.***

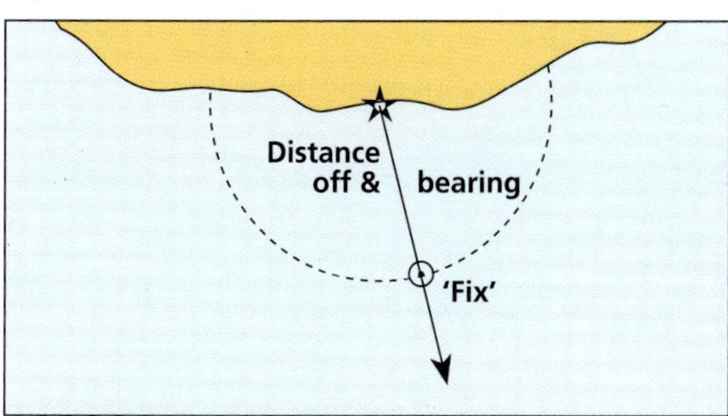

A bearing of the object and its distance off provide a 'Fix'.

Taking a vertical sextant angle (VSA)

(On a lighthouse)

Hold the sextant vertically, set the index to zero and view the centre of the light through the telescope. The True image will be seen through the plain half of the horizon glass and the reflected image in the mirror half *Fig 1*.

Both images should coincide. Turn the micrometer drum so that the index bar moves along the arc away from you and the image will separate, the reflected image moving downward. Tilt the sextant to follow this movement until the centre of the light reaches the shore line. Read the angle and correct for index error *Fig 2*.

Refer the corrected angle and the charted height of the light to the table on *page 134* or to the appropriate table in the Almanac to obtain a 'distance off'. Couple this with a bearing of the light taken at the same time as the sextant angle to obtain a 'fix' by bearing and distance.

NOTE The height of terrestrial objects is measured from the level of MHWS. If the sea level is below this datum when the sextant angle is taken, the apparent height of the object is increased which also increases the angle being measured. This gives the impression that the boat is closer to the object than it actually is, and provides a slight 'safety margin'.

Vertical sextant angles

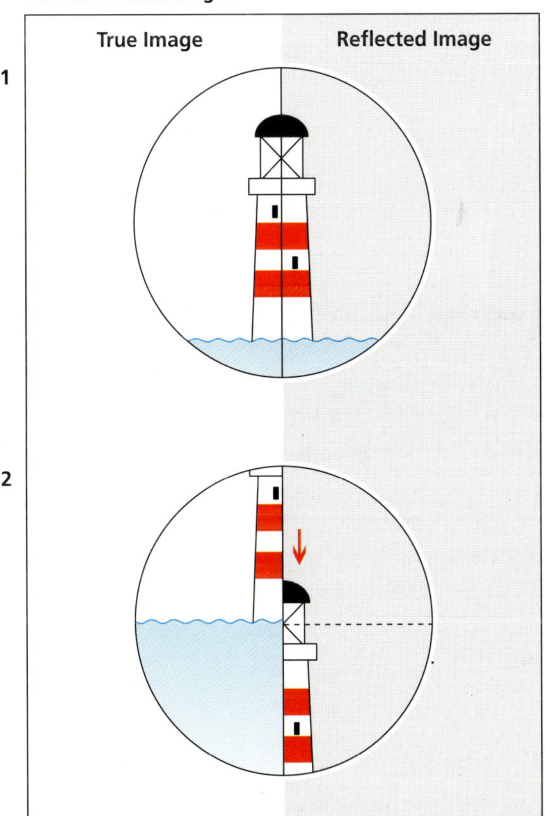

NOTE If an almanac or tables are unavailable the distance off by vertical sextant angle can be found by using the formula:

$$\textbf{Distance off (nm)} = \frac{\textbf{1.852 x height in metres}}{\textbf{angle in minutes of arc}}$$

Horizontal sextant angles

(between three objects)

To prevent erroneous results when three objects are being observed, they should all lie on or close to the same straight line or the centre object should be nearer to the observer than the other two.

Hold the sextant horizontally, handle down, with index set to zero.

View the centre object through the telescope, *Fig 1* and, using the quick release lever, move the index bar along the arc so that the reflected image B moves to the left.

Swing the sextant to keep the image in view until it approaches the left hand object A, *Fig 2*.

Make the final adjustment using the micrometer drum until the reflected image B is superimposed upon the true image A, *Fig 3*.

Read the angle and correct for index error and repeat the procedure between objects B and C.

1

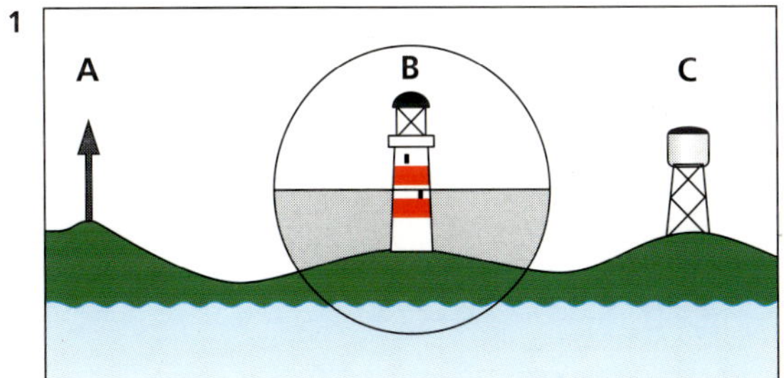
A
B
C

2

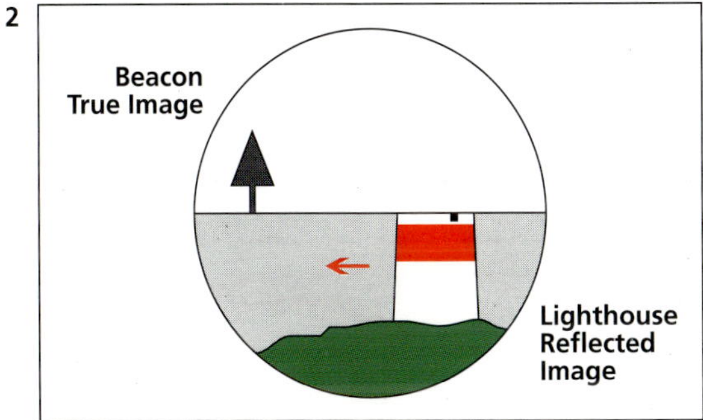
Beacon
True Image
Lighthouse
Reflected
Image

3

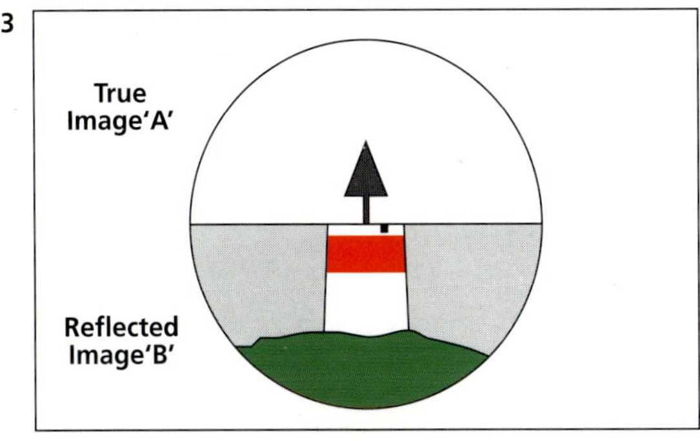
True
Image'A'
Reflected
Image'B'

Fix by horizontal angle to three marks

Example:-

Three marks are sighted A, B and C.

The first angle between A and B is 40°.

The second angle between B and C is 25°.

On the Chart

1 Join position A to B and B to C with straight lines.

2 Subtract each angle taken from 90° to produce angles of 50° and 65° respectively.

3 From position A draw a line towards the observer making an angle of 50° with line A-B and another line from position B also at an angle of 50° so that both lines cross at point D.

4 Repeat this procedure for positions B and C using the second angle 65° so that the lines cross at point E.

5 With D as centre draw a circle which passes through both positions A and B.

6 With E as centre draw a circle which passes through both positions B and C.

7 The observer's position lies at the intersection of the circles - point X.

Plotting the horizontal angle fix

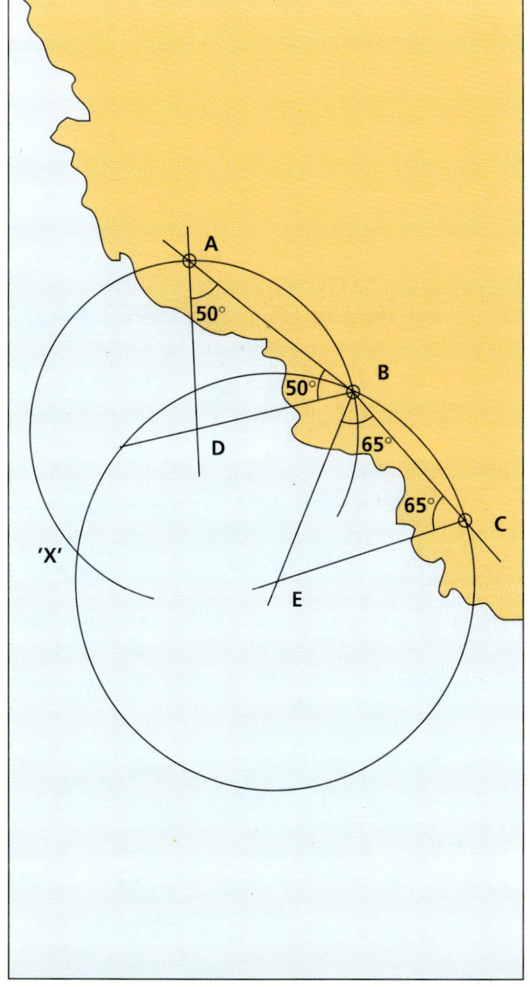

An approximate 'distance off' may be obtained at night when approaching land by observing the point at which a light first appears above the horizon or conversely when leaving the coast by noting the point at which it is on the verge of disappearing below the horizon.

This distance, which is dependant upon the 'height of eye' of the observer and the elevation of the light is called the Geographical Range of the light and is the maximum distance at which a light with sufficient intensity can be seen when limited only by the curvature of the Earth.

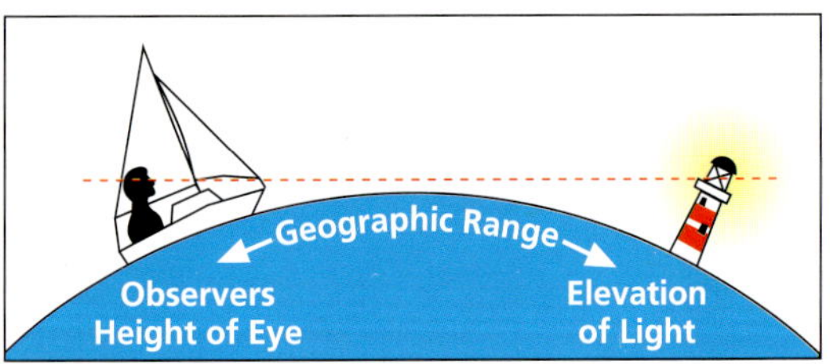

The observed height of the light above sea level together with the height of eye of the observer is referred to in the Geographical Range table in the Almanac to obtain the 'distance off.'

By rising or dipping of lights

1. Charted height of light	
2. plus level of MHWS	
3. is – height of light above Chart Datum	
4. minus height of tide prevailing	
5. is – height of light above sea level	

Refer height of light found and the observer's height of eye to the range of light table to obtain the distance off. A bearing of the light taken at the same time will provide the remaining information to obtain a reliable fix.

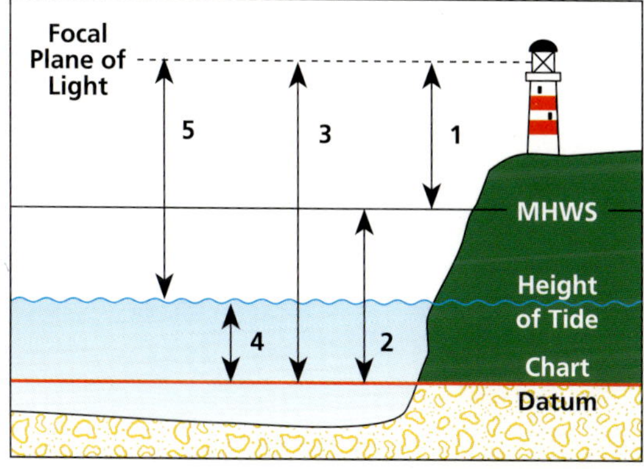

The 'air draught' or clearance under a bridge or cables which cross a navigable waterway is usually clearly marked on large scale charts of the area. The clearance given is measured from the level of MHWS at that place, *Fig 1*.

The water level under a bridge will seldom be as high as this so the clearance is usually greater than that indicated. It should be remembered however, that the water level in estuaries and rivers may be raised substantially by strong on-shore winds, heavy rainfall, or by the relief of weirs upstream and for these reasons a good margin for error should be allowed.

1

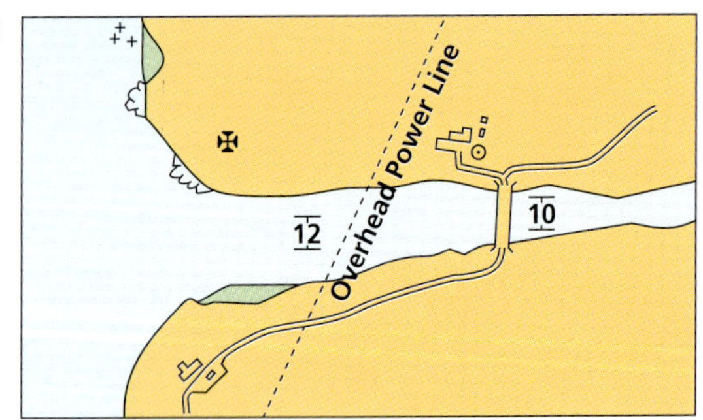

Will my vessel clear?

1. Charted height of the bridge	
2. plus level of MHWS	
3. is – bridge height above Chart Datum	
4. minus present height of tide	
5. is – bridge height above sea level	
6. minus mast height above waterline	
7. is – clearance (if any) below bridge	

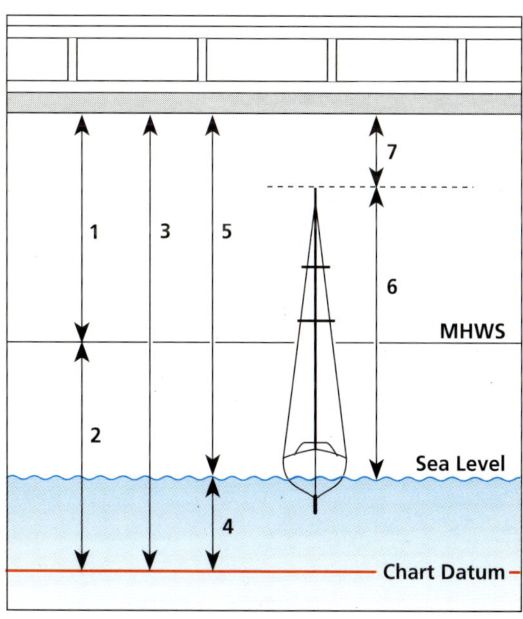

General conduct in any condition of visibility

Always maintain a proper lookout.
Adjust speed to suit prevailing conditions.
Know who has right of way.

Remember

Risk of collision exists if the bearing of converging vessels remains constant or nearly so.

Vessels with Right of Way

Hold a steady course and speed but be prepared to stop or turn away if the other vessel fails to take action.

Give Way Vessel

Take early, positive and obvious avoiding action. Do not cross ahead of the other vessel.

IMPORTANT NOTE This abridged interpretation of parts A and B of the rules must only be used in conjunction with the complete regulations.

Power driven vessels

including vessels sailing and simultaneously using engines.

When Crossing

Vessel with another on her own starboard side gives way and avoids crossing ahead.

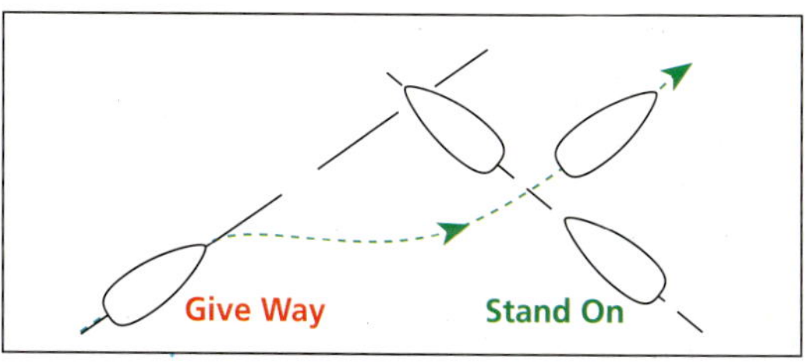

Meeting Head On

BOTH vessels turn to starboard.

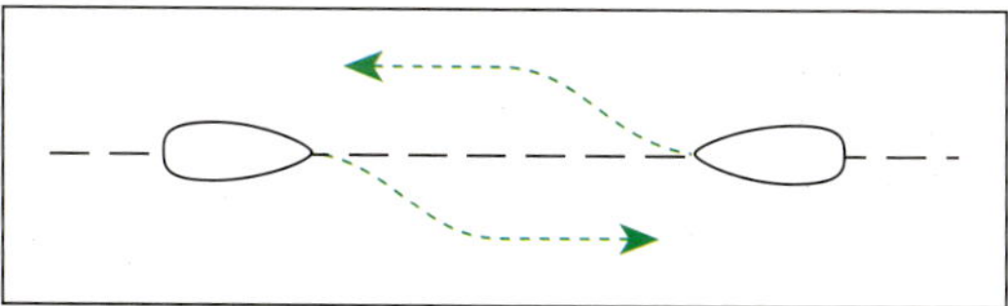

Overtaking

Keeps clear of other vessel.

Power Driven Vessels Keep Clear Of

Sailing vessels. *Not using power.*

Vessels engaged in fishing.

Vessels not under command (*unable to comply with the rules*).

Vessels restricted in their ability to manoeuvre or hampered by their draught.

Sailing vessels

Vessels with Wind on Opposite Sides

The vessel on **Port Tack** gives way.

Vessels with Wind on the Same Side

The **Windward** boat gives way.

NOTE A vessel with wind on her port side, which is unable to determine which tack a boat to windward of her is on, should make preparation to give way.

Overtaking

All vessels, sail or power driven when overtaking from astern are responsible for keeping clear 'until past and clear'.

Sailing Vessels (not using power) Keep Clear Of

Vessels engaged in fishing.

Vessels not under command *(unable to comply with the rules)*.

Vessels restricted in their ability to manoeuvre or hampered by their draught.

Sailing vessels meeting

Right of way

A On Port Tack
Keeps clear of B
Keeps clear of C
Keeps clear of D

B On Starboard Tack
Keeps clear of D
Stands on for A
Stands on for C

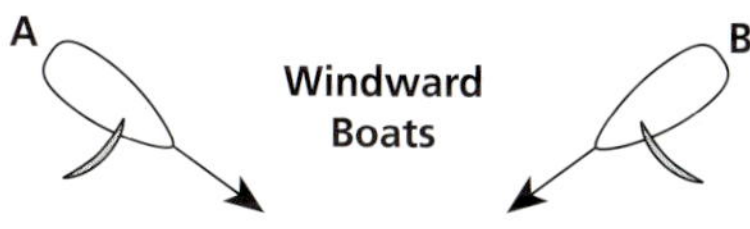

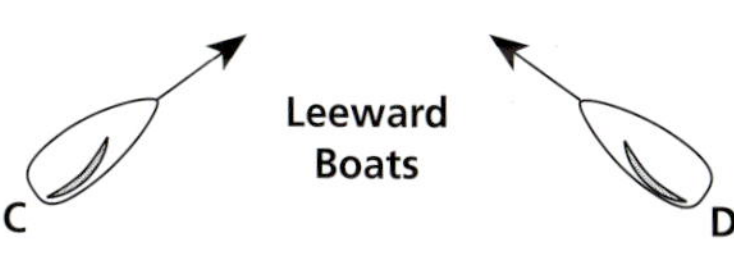

C On Port Tack
Keeps clear of B
Keeps clear of D
Stands on for A

D On Starboard Tack
Stands on for A
Stands on for B
Stands on for C

Lights must be shown from sunset to sunrise and at all times during reduced visibility. Colours and cut off angles of lights are designed to indicate the type of vessel and direction of travel.

Definitions and Arcs of Visibility

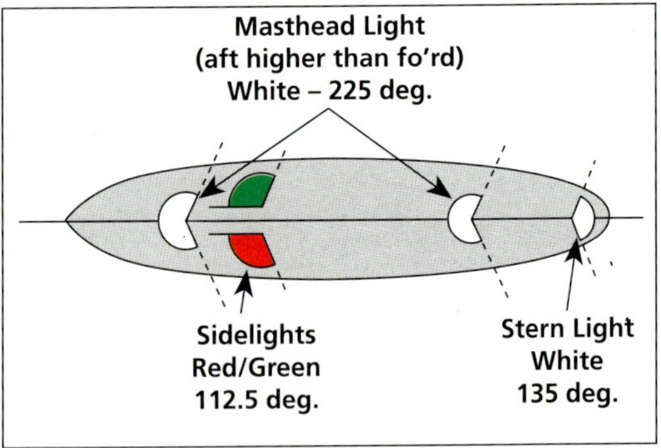

All round Light

Shows an unbroken light over an arc of 360°.

Flashing Light

Regular flashes of 120 or more per minute.

Towing Light

A yellow light with the same characteristics as a stern light and mounted above it.

Blue Lights

Are carried by Police and Customs vessels on duty.

Lights required for Motor Yachts

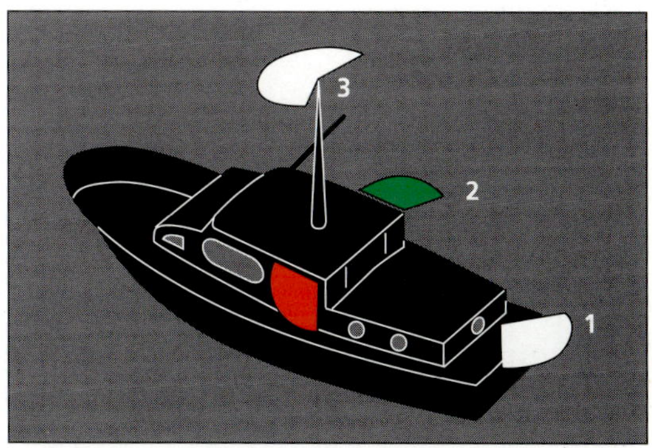

Vessels 12 to 20m LOA

1 A white stern light.

2 Red and green sidelights mounted separately or combined in a single bi-lantern.

3 A white masthead light shown at least 2·5m above the level of the sidelights.

Vessels under 12m LOA

Must carry stern and side lights as specified above and a masthead light mounted a least 1m above the level of the side lights.

Vessels under 7m LOA

Maximum speed not exceeding 7kt

Required to carry a single all round white light but should also carry sidelights if practicable to do so.

Sailing vessels under 20m

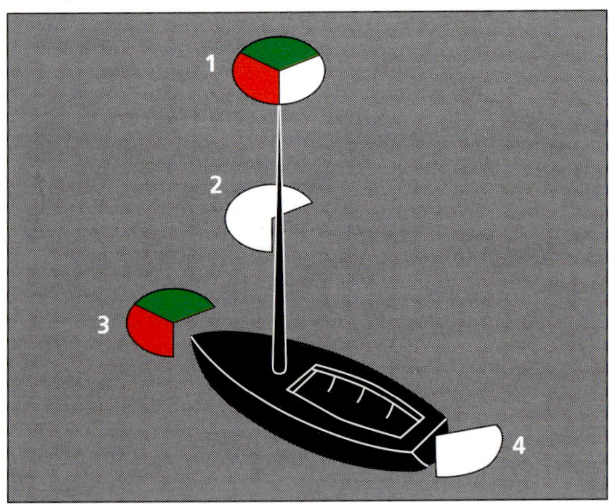

Sailing Vessels Not Using Power –
show lanterns 1 or 3 and 4.

Optional 'ALL ROUND' red over green masthead lights may also be shown with lanterns 3 and 4 but NOT in conjunction with lantern 1, or when using auxiliary power.

Sailing Vessels Using Power –
show lantern 2, 3 and 4.

When using sail AND power together by day, all vessels MUST exhibit a black cone point down in the fore-part where best seen.

Vessels Under 7m in Length –

If unable to exhibit these lights MUST have a white light ready to display to avoid collision.

Hovercraft and Hydrofoils

Normal lights for power driven vessels and an all round flashing yellow light when in non-displacement mode.

Vessels Towing

Two masthead lights forward in a vertical line or if the length of tow exceeds 200m - three lights in a vertical line. Also side lights, stern light and a yellow light mounted above the stern light.

Vessel Towed

Stern and sidelights only.

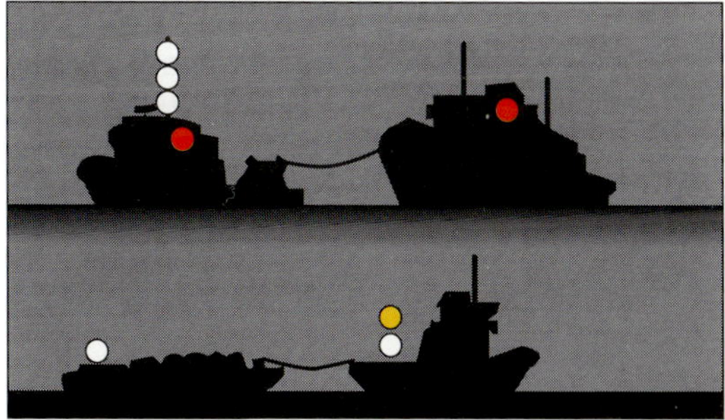

By Day: *When length of tow is over 200m both vessels display a diamond shape.*

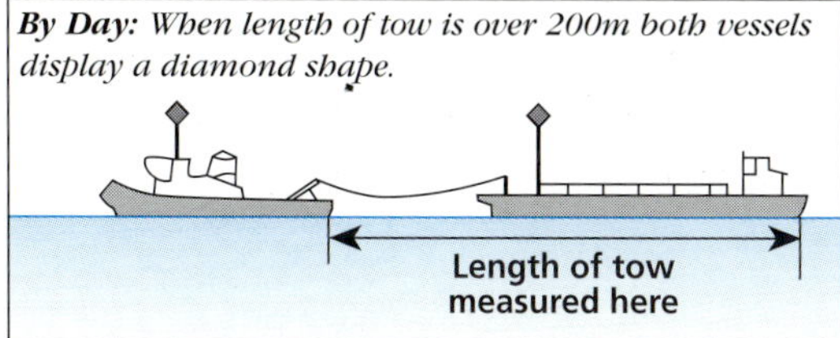

Vessel Constrained by Draught

Three all round red lights with normal navigation lights when making way.

By Day: *Shows a black cylinder.*

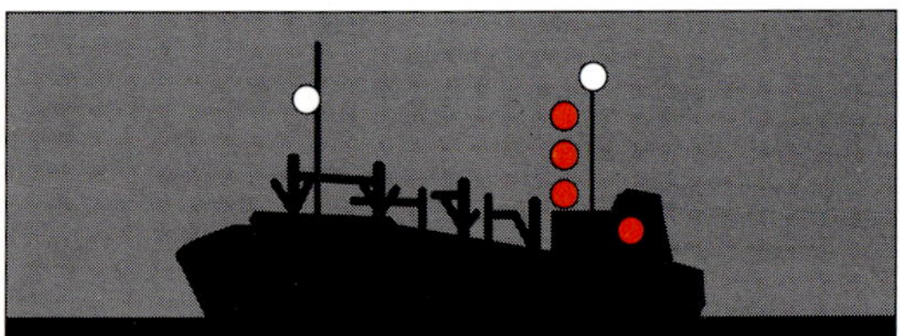

Vessel Not Under Command

(Unable to comply with the rules)

Two all round red lights and when making way – stern and sidelights.

By Day: *Two black balls in vertical line.*

Vessel Aground

Two all round red lights and anchor lights.

By Day: *Three black balls.*

Vessels Trawling

Two all round lights green over white and lights for a power driven vessel underway.

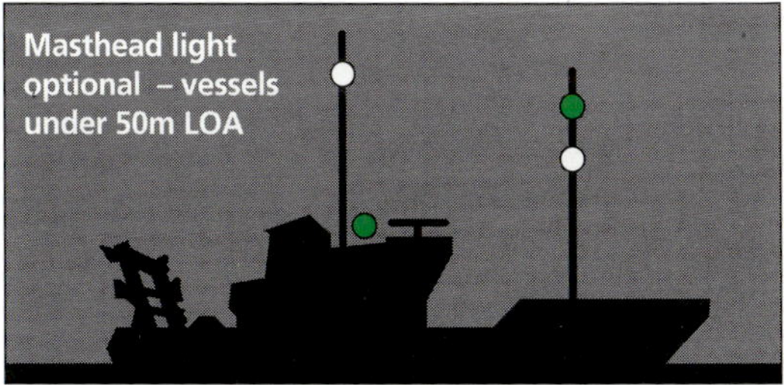

Pair Trawling

Vessels trawling as a pair direct searchlights forward and toward one another.

Vessel Fishing (other than trawling)

Two all round lights red over white plus stern and sidelights when under way.

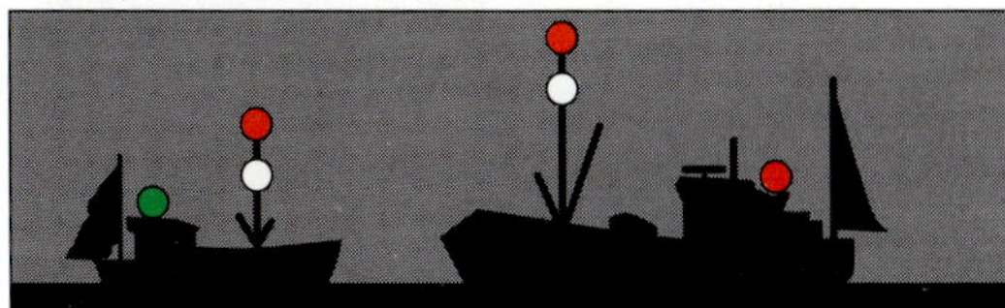

By Day: Shows a shape – two cones apex together.
Additional signals: *F/V in close proximity*
Trawler hauling nets: ○ **Shooting nets:** ○
two all round lights ● *two all round lights* ○
Vessel using Purse Seine Gear:
alternate flashing yellow

Vessels Restricted in Ability to Manoeuvre

Three all round lights - red/white/red in a vertical line and masthead - stern and sidelights when making way.
By Day: *Shows a ball over a diamond over a ball (Fig 1).*

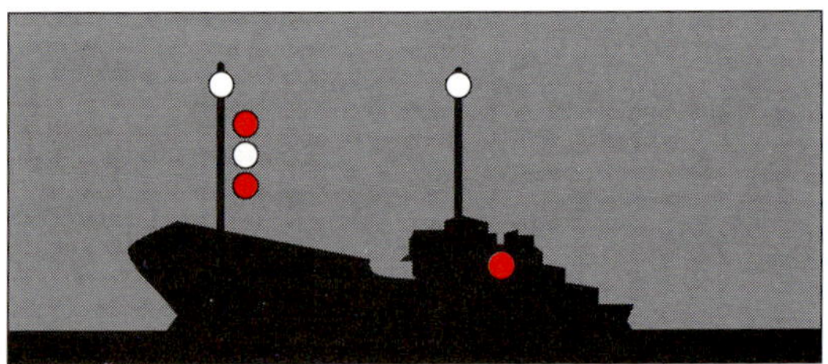

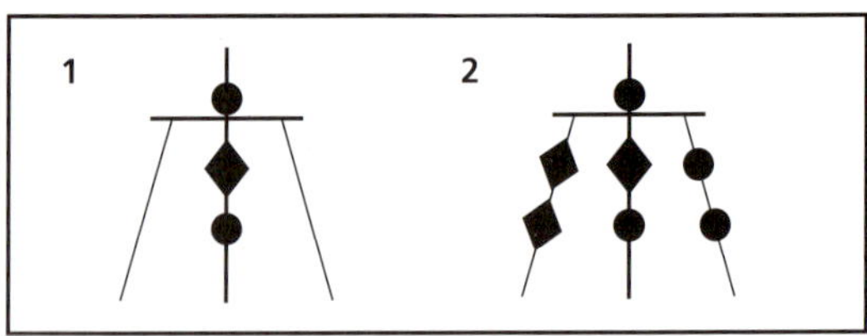

Vessels Engaged in Underwater Operations or Dredging

When making way also shows masthead, stern and sidelights. If anchored does **not** *show anchor lights.*
By Day: *Shows a black ball over a diamond over a ball, on the obstructed side two balls, on the clear side two diamonds (Fig 2).*

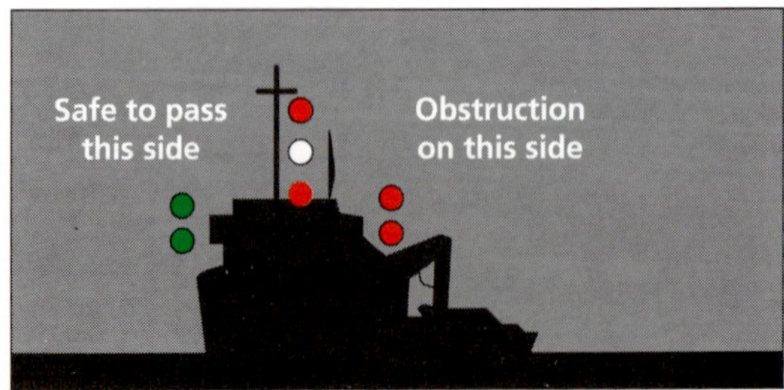

Vessels Minesweeping

Three all round green lights with normal navigation lights.

Dangerous to approach closer than 1000m astern or 500m on either side.

By Day: *All round green lights are replaced by black balls.*

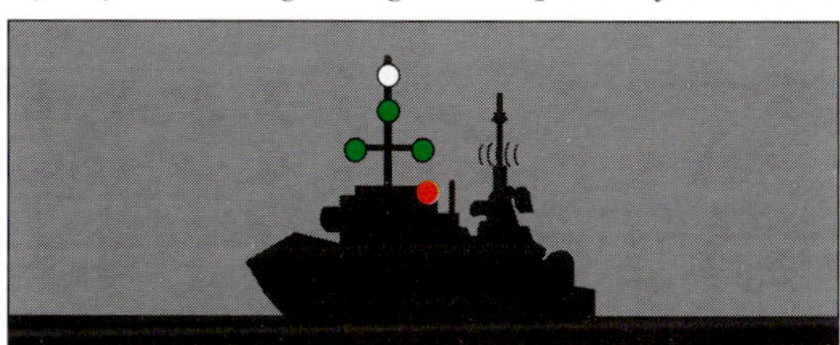

Pilot Vessel: On Duty

Two all round lights white over red and stern and sidelights when making way. At anchor shows an anchor light.

By Day: *Flies a white and red flag.*

Vessel at Anchor

By Day: *Shows a black sphere.*

Vessels more than 100m LOA must also illuminate their decks.

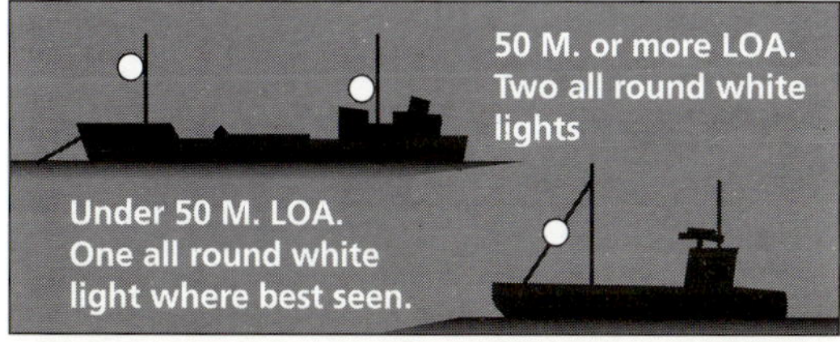

50 M. or more LOA.
Two all round white lights
Under 50 M. LOA.
One all round white light where best seen.

These are displayed by day in various combinations and in all weathers to indicate certain activities in which the vessel carrying them is engaged.

In conditions of reduced visibility the appropriate lights may also be shown.

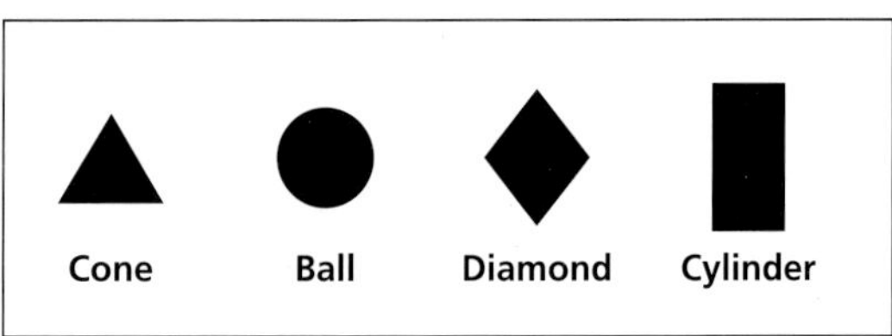

A vessel is deemed to be UNDER WAY when not at anchor or moored to the shore and is MAKING WAY when being propelled through the water by any means of propulsion.

IMPORTANT NOTE This abridged interpretation of part C of The Rules must only be used in conjunction with the complete regulations.

Horn or whistle

Short Blast ●   Long Blast ▬

Vessels Manoeuvring

Turning to Starboard	●
Turning to Port	● ●
Engines in reverse	● ● ●
Alert "Wake up"	● ● ● ● ●

Vessel in Narrow Channel

Nearing blind bends	▬
Intent to overtake:	
to Starboard	▬ ▬ ●
to Port	▬ ▬ ● ●
Agreement by other vessel	▬ ● ▬ ●

During Poor Visibility (Day or night)

Sounded at two minute intervals

Power vessel making way

Under way but **not** making way

Not under command Unable to manoeuvre Hampered by draught Vessel fishing Vessel towing/pushing Sailing vessel (not using power)	▬ ● ●

Vessel under tow (If manned)	▬ ● ● ●

Vessels at anchor or aground (in poor visibility)

At Anchor

Vessels under 100m in length must ring a bell for 5sec every minute.

A vessel 100m or more in length must ring a bell 'forward' for 5sec every minute immediately followed by a gong sounded for 5sec 'aft'.

Any vessel at anchor may also give a warning of collision to an approaching vessel by sounding morse 'R' (· — ·) on a horn.

Vessels Aground

Signals as for at anchor but preceded and followed by 3 separate and distinct bell strokes.

Vessels Under 12m in length

May make the appropriate sound signals given above or MUST make some other efficient sound signal at intervals of not less than 2 min.

IMPORTANT NOTE To be read in conjunction with the complete list given in the International Regulations for Preventing Collision at Sea.

IALA Maritime Buoyage System

Lateral Marks: Used in the conventional direction of buoyage to define the limits of navigable channels in the general direction of harbour from seaward.

Bifurcation Marks (Modified lateral marks): Used to mark the point where a channel divides when proceeding in the conventional direction of buoyage and to indicate the main or preferred channel.

Isolated Danger Mark: Used to indicate an isolated danger of limited size which has navigable water all around it.

Safe Water Mark: Used as a centre channel or landfall mark with deep navigable water all around it.

Cardinal Marks: Cover the four quadrants N, S, E & W. Each mark is named after the quadrant it guards and indicates the side upon which it should be passed in safety, i.e. pass to the North of a North Cardinal.

Special Marks: Used to mark areas of particular interest such as spoil grounds, water sport or military exercise areas etc. Marks can be any shape and are not primarily intended to assist navigation but if the marks are either cone or can shape, it is advisable to regard them as lateral marks and treat them accordingly.

Cardinal Marks

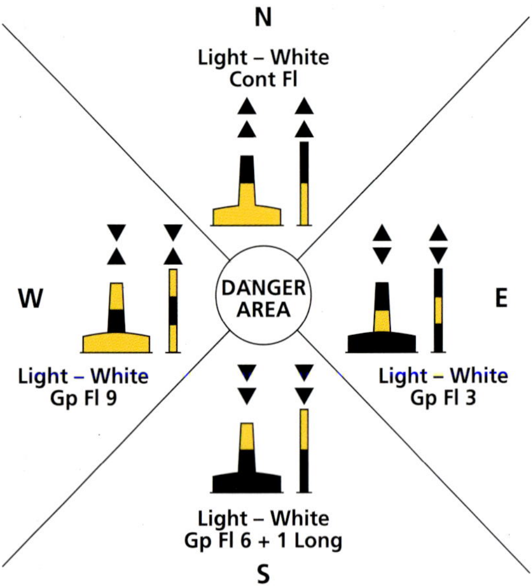

N

Light – White
Cont Fl

W

Light – White
Gp Fl 9

DANGER
AREA

E

Light – White
Gp Fl 3

Light – White
Gp Fl 6 + 1 Long

S

Isolated Danger Mark

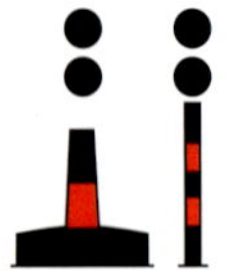

Danger with safe water all round
Light – White GP Fl 2

Safe Water Mark

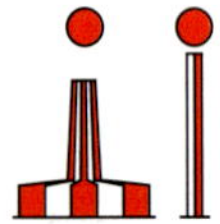

Safe deep water
Light – White
Occulting – Isophase –
or 1 long flash

Lateral Marks – Region 'A'

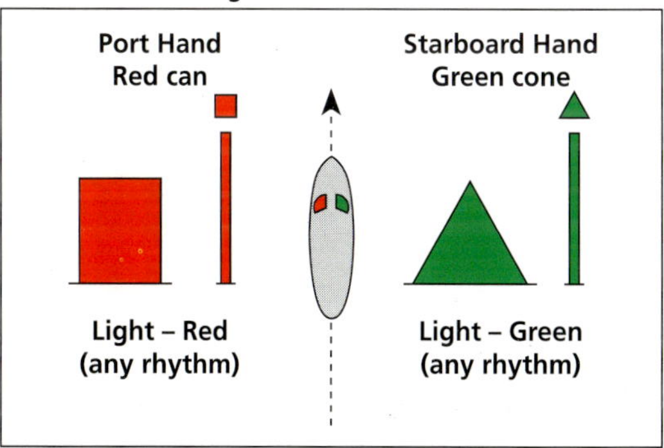

Bifurcation Marks *(Modified Lateral Marks)*

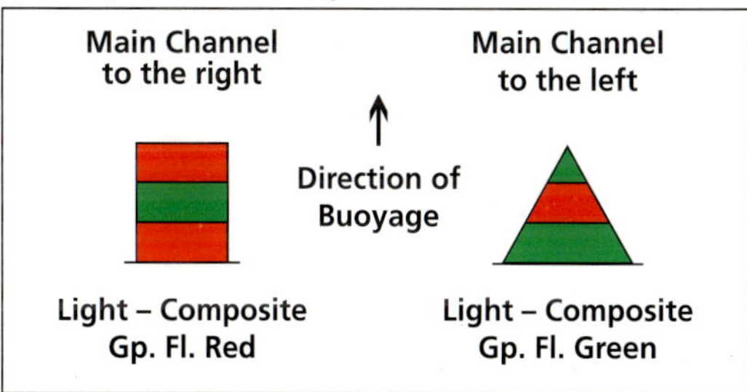

Special Marks *(any shape - Yellow)*

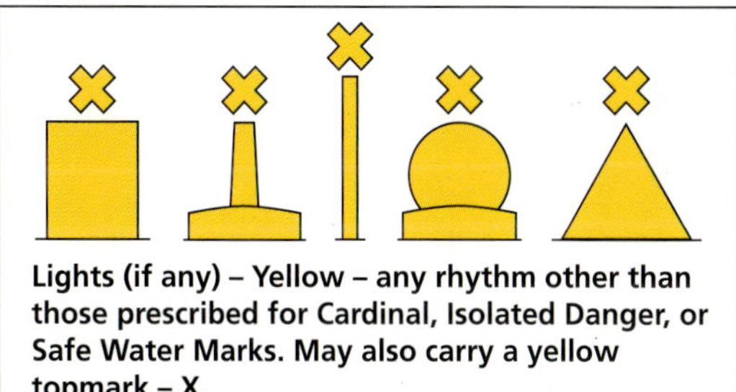

Lights (if any) – Yellow – any rhythm other than those prescribed for Cardinal, Isolated Danger, or Safe Water Marks. May also carry a yellow topmark – X.

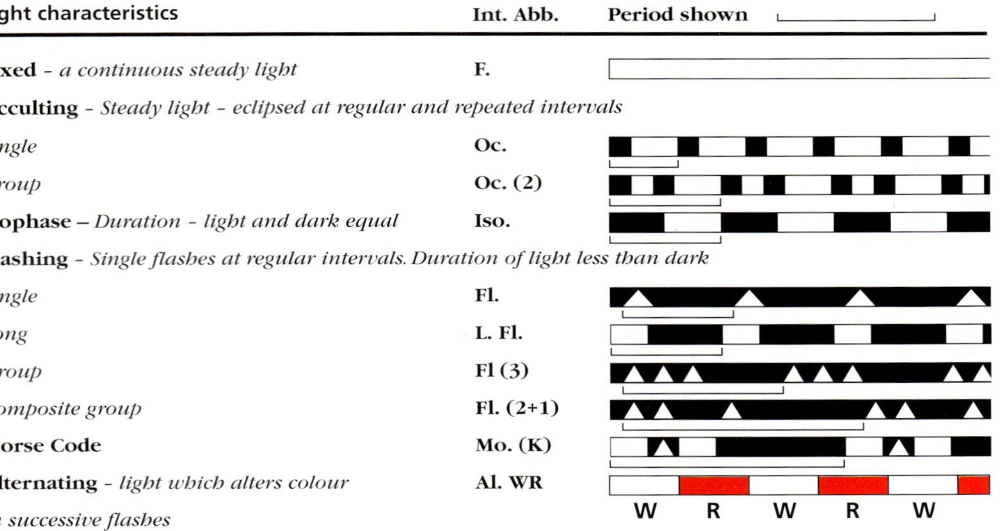

Light characteristics	Int. Abb.	Period shown
Fixed – *a continuous steady light*	**F.**	
Occulting – *Steady light – eclipsed at regular and repeated intervals*		
Single	**Oc.**	
Group	**Oc. (2)**	
Isophase – *Duration – light and dark equal*	**Iso.**	
Flashing – *Single flashes at regular intervals. Duration of light less than dark*		
Single	**Fl.**	
Long	**L. Fl.**	
Group	**Fl (3)**	
Composite group	**Fl. (2+1)**	
Morse Code	**Mo. (K)**	
Alternating – *light which alters colour in successive flashes*	**Al. WR**	

Safety at sea begins with a well-found boat and a competent skipper and crew. In addition all craft should carry the safety equipment which is recommended or required by the DOT for that particular vessel. The full list which is given in the almanac includes such essentials as:- Navigation Lights, Radar Reflector, Fire Extinguishers, Fog Horn, Lifebuoys, First Aid Kit, Life Jacket and Harness for each crew member, Life-raft or equivalent, and a Flare Pack.

White flares are NOT a distress signal they are used to warn others of danger of collision.

Red flares or Orange smoke signify distress.

Red flares and VHF radio are the mariner's principle means of signalling distress. All flares carry instructions for their correct use, make sure that you know how to use them BEFORE you need them and that they are still within their expiry date.

A VHF radio will keep you in touch and enable you to send or receive distress or urgency messages, contact Coastguard or Harbour Authorities, and receive the latest weather forecast.

Safety-conscious skippers will also join the Coastguard Small Craft Safety Scheme which gives them early warning of overdue vessels. It costs nothing and details are available from HM Coastguard.

Some other Recognised Signals for help

Morse letters SOS by any means. Continuous sounding of fog horn. Ball shape over or under a square shape. Slowly raising and lowering both arms. Letters NC by flag or morse code.

Distress or Emergency signals (VHF)

Only to be used when there is grave and imminent danger to a vessel or person and immediate assistance is required.

SWITCH ON THE RADIO - SELECT CHANNEL 16
TRANSMIT ON HIGH POWER

Mayday – Mayday – Mayday

This is – Name of vessel – three times

Mayday – Name of vessel once

Give your Position

State the Nature of the Emergency
(And type of assistance required)

Give any other helpful Information

Mayday – Over

If the emergency does not warrant a full Mayday alert (or if in doubt) the URGENCY call may be used instead.

SWITCH ON THE RADIO - SELECT CHANNEL 16
TRANSMIT ON HIGH POWER

PanPan – PanPan – PanPan

All stations – All stations – All stations

This is – Vessels name three times

Give your Position

State nature of the Emergency
(And type of assistance required)

Over

A	ALPHA
B	BRAVO
C	CHARLIE
D	DELTA
E	ECHO
F	FOXTROT
G	GOLF
H	HOTEL
I	INDIA
J	JULIET
K	KILO
L	LIMA
M	MIKE
N	NOVEMBER
O	OSCAR
P	PAPA
Q	QUEBEC
R	ROMEO
S	SIERRA
T	TANGO
U	UNIFORM
V	VICTOR
W	WHISKEY
X	X-RAY
Y	YANKEE
Z	ZULU

International code of signals

Communication between vessels nowadays is usually carried out by radio, but code signals may also be sent by flag, light, or sound.

Single letter signals are perhaps the most important of code signals and are understood internationally. Each letter of the alphabet except R is a complete message when sent individually i.e.

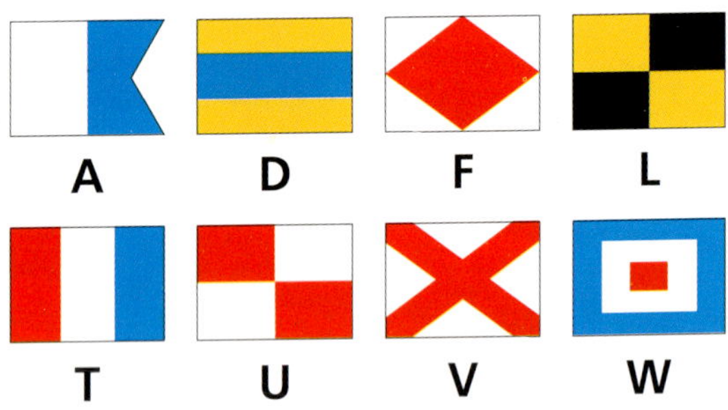

A I have a diver down. Keep clear.

D Keep clear. Manoeuvring with difficulty.

F I am disabled. Communicate with me.

L You should stop your vessel instantly.

T Keep clear - Pair trawling.

U You are running into danger.

V I require assistance.

W I require medical assistance.

A list of signals is reproduced in most nautical almanacs.

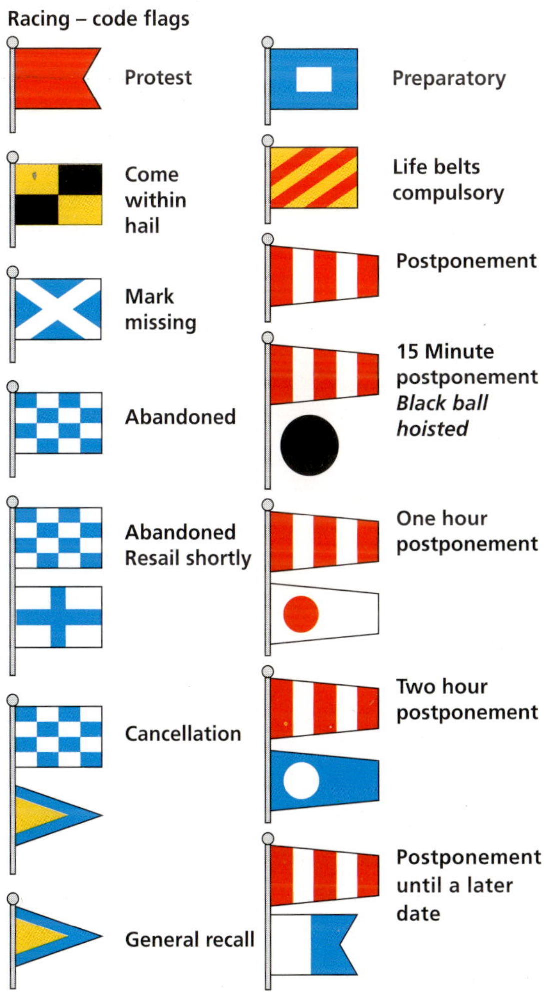

The meaning of single letter code flags when used for racing purposes.

A	● ▬
B	▬ ● ● ●
C	▬ ● ▬ ●
D	▬ ● ●
E	●
F	● ● ▬ ●
G	▬ ▬ ●
H	● ● ● ●
I	● ●
J	● ▬ ▬ ▬
K	▬ ● ▬
L	● ▬ ● ●
M	▬ ▬
N	▬ ●
O	▬ ▬ ▬
P	● ▬ ▬ ●
Q	▬ ▬ ● ▬
R	● ▬ ●
S	● ● ●
T	▬
U	● ● ▬
V	● ● ● ▬
W	● ▬ ▬
X	▬ ● ● ▬
Y	▬ ● ▬ ▬
Z	▬ ▬ ● ●
1	● ▬ ▬ ▬ ▬
2	● ● ▬ ▬ ▬
3	● ● ● ▬ ▬
4	● ● ● ● ▬
5	● ● ● ● ●
6	▬ ● ● ● ●
7	▬ ▬ ● ● ●
8	▬ ▬ ▬ ● ●
9	▬ ▬ ▬ ▬ ●
0	▬ ▬ ▬ ▬ ▬

A summary

Weather as we know it is the direct result of changes in temperature within the moist dense air mass that envelops the Earth. The air exerts a pressure on the surface of the earth and atmospheric pressure at sea level measured by barometer averages 1013·2mb, but radiant energy from the sun heats the surface unevenly so that the atmosphere is warmer in some places than in others and since warm air is less dense than cold air it rises - cold air sinks to replace it - and variations above and below average pressure occur resulting in regions of relatively high and low pressure. Air always moves from a region of high pressure to one of lower pressure - but not directly because the movement is deflected by the rotation of the Earth. The flow of air is felt as wind whenever there is a difference in atmospheric pressure between two localities and its strength is determined by the rate of change in pressure between the two centres.

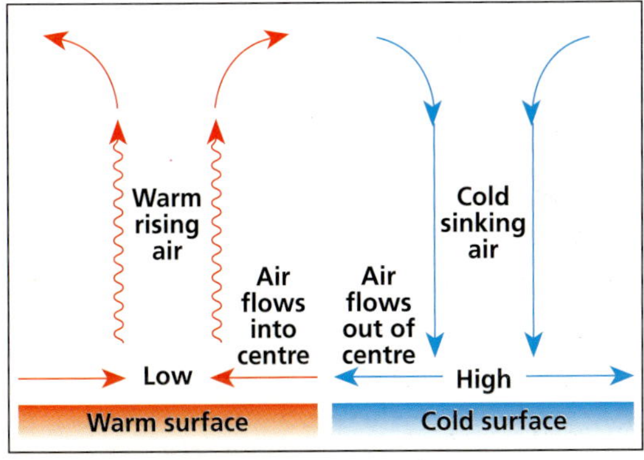

Wind belts

This global convection process which results in a pattern of pressure and wind belts around the earth also occurs on a smaller scale all over the world. Generally, when air is moving down in an area of high pressure, the weather is dry and settled, but where the air is rising and pressure is low the weather is disturbed because rising air cools, expands and condenses into cloud and this rising air draws in more of the surrounding air masses to fuel the process.

Variation in barometric pressure is one of the mariner's principle indications of impending changes to wind and weather in the vicinity.

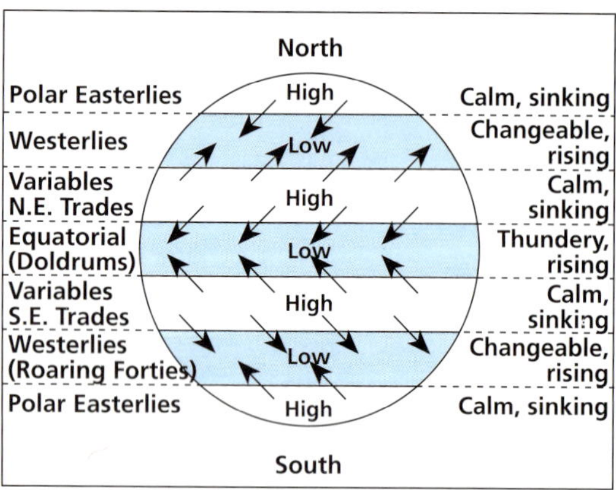

General circulation of the atmosphere for rotating earth.

Highs and Lows

Anticyclones and depressions (highs and lows) are the two main weather systems of the middle latitudes. In the northern hemisphere an anticyclone is a system where winds blow in a clockwise direction around areas of high pressure. The strongest winds blow round the outer extremities of the area and gradually diminish in strength toward the centre where they are light or non-existent. Anticyclones are fair weather systems with moderate winds and reasonably clear skies. They are generally slow moving, sometimes remaining stationary for several days.

Depressions and their associated fronts are largely responsible for unsettled weather, strong winds and heavy rainfall. A depression is an area of low pressure around which the winds blow in an anti-clockwise direction in the northern hemisphere. They vary greatly in size and intensity and can move rapidly in any direction but most usually eastward.

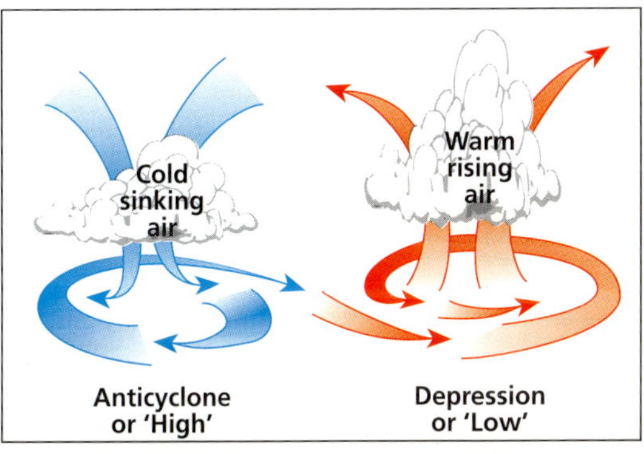

Fronts

A 'Front' is the boundary between two kinds of air. The main air masses which affect British waters originate from either the Polar or Sub-tropical Highs. Although classified according to its source, each air mass may arrive by different routes, therefore its properties will depend upon its path and the general kind of weather to be expected from each mass is:

Arctic and Polar - Cold

Tropical - Warm

Maritime - Wet

Continental - Dry

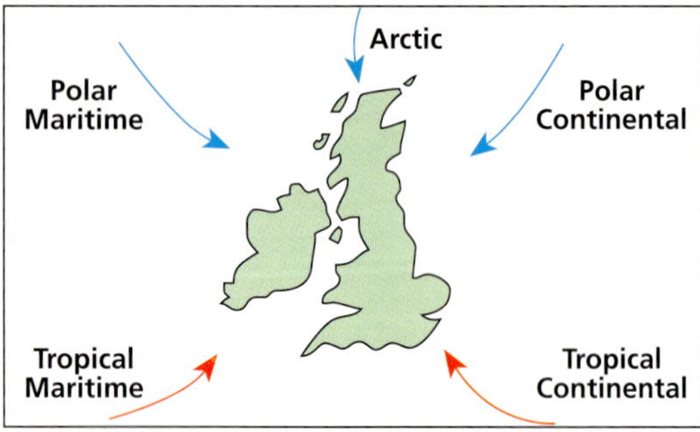

Most depressions that approach Britain form along the Polar Front - the name given to the boundary between these two air masses.

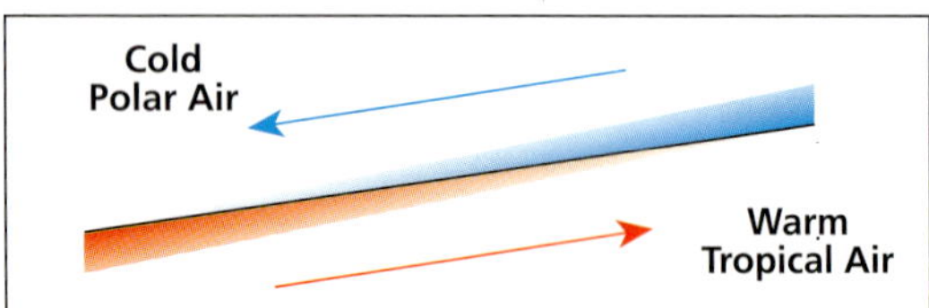

Front with opposing air currents.

Depressions

When warm and cold air masses meet they interact and a wave develops in the front with its tip on the pole-ward side. Atmospheric pressure at the tip of the wave commences to fall until a complete circulation of air around a low pressure centre is established and a sector of warm air has become trapped in a squeeze between the cold air behind and the cool air ahead producing the fronts which are characteristic of a depression.

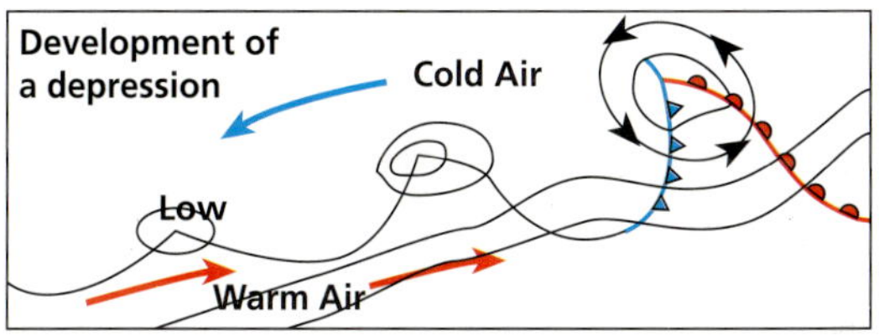

Depressions are bad weather systems with their most turbulent winds occurring at their centres, therefore it is always advantageous to know where the centre of an approaching depression lies in relation to one's own position.

BUYS BALLOT'S LAW states that if you face the wind in the northern hemisphere the low pressure centre will be between 90°-135° on your right hand side. 'The Crossed Winds' rule also provides a rough guide to weather trends if you face the wind and look up at the clouds to compare the direction of the higher altitude wind. If the cloud comes from the right the weather is likely to deteriorate. If the movement is from the left, the weather will most likely improve, but if the movement is either directly toward or away from you, then existing conditions will probably remain unchanged.

Maps

A weather map shows the distribution of atmospheric pressure throughout an area by means of lines - Isobars - drawn through places having the same pressure. The isobaric structure in any area gives an indication of the weather pattern prevailing there, i.e. isobars are drawn at intervals of 2, 4, or 8mb either side of 1000mb thus forming a pressure contour map similar to a geographical contour map. The pressure gradient is the rate of change in pressure across the isobars and is analogous to the gradient of a hill. Closely spaced land contours indicate steep gradients, similarly, closely spaced isobars portray steep pressure gradients which, in turn, produce stronger winds *Fig 1*.

1

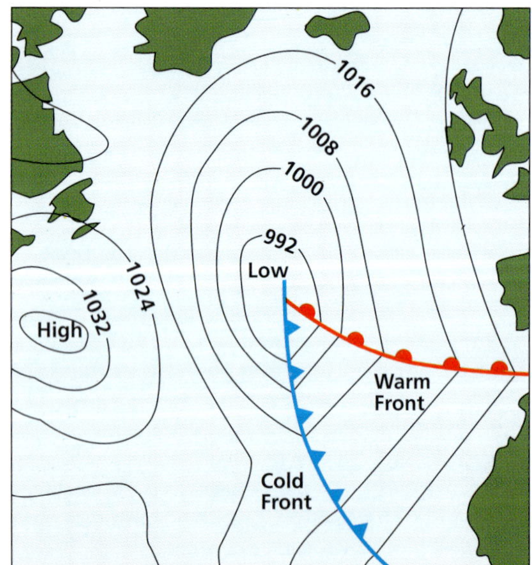

Each isobar forms a closed circuit around a centre of either high or low pressure and in the northern hemisphere, winds above 2000ft blow parallel to the isobars - clockwise around areas of high pressure and anti-clockwise around low pressure areas. Surface winds however are always 'backed' from the direction of the isobars and diverge away from a centre of high pressure but converge toward a centre of low pressure *Fig 2*.

2

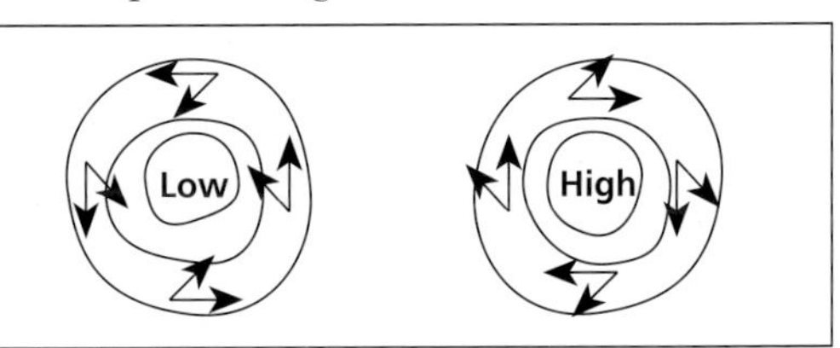

(Verifying Buys Ballot's Law, see page 121)

Fig 3 depicts a simple depression in the northern hemisphere with winds blowing anti-clockwise in the general direction of the isobars but backed slightly inwards. From the centre, line A-B represents the warm front - the leading edge of the air in the warm sector which is riding up over the relatively cold air to the right of it. Line A-C is the cold front. This is the leading edge of a wedge of cold air which is pushing into the warm sector ahead of it. In this instance the depression and its fronts are moving steadily from left to right in the general direction of the isobars in the warm sector and an observer stationed at 'X' might expect to experience the following pattern of events as the depression passes over him.

High cloud from the west increases and lowers as the warm front approaches, pressure falls and the wind strengthens and backs, visibility deteriorates and light rain becomes continuous and heavy. As the warm front passes, pressure steadies, the wind veers, and rain stops or turns to drizzle. In the warm sector, visibility is poor with drizzle or showers. Wind and pressure is steady. At the cold front, pressure falls then rises sharply. Wind veers and becomes squally with heavy rain. As the front moves away, rain stops, visibility improves, and pressure rises.

3

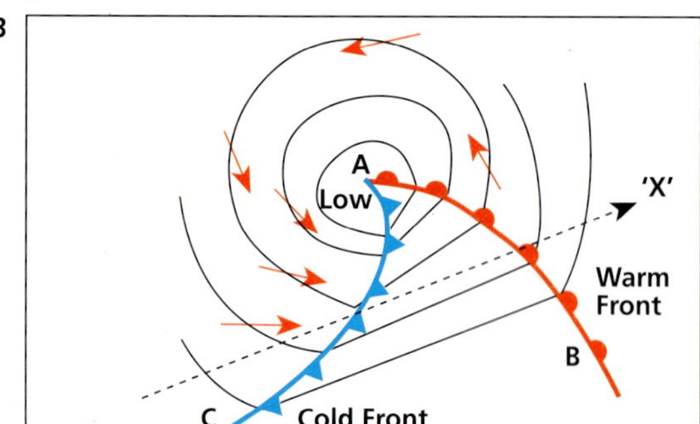

4

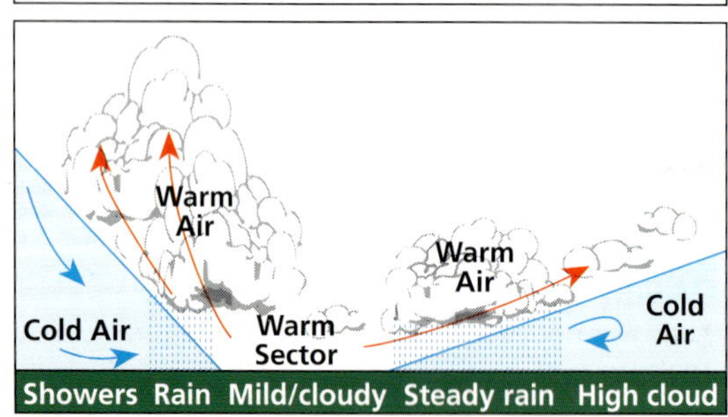

Section through a warm sector depression.

Local effects

Wind is moving air created by temperature differences. Local winds in various forms are a modification to the general weather pattern but stem from the same basic cause.

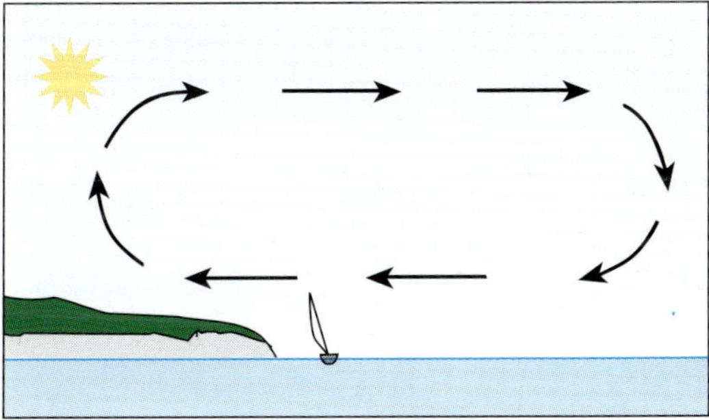

Sea Breezes *develop in coastal areas when convection over the land on a warm sunny day causes strong up currents of air. The rising air is replaced by an inflow of air from over the sea which creates an onshore wind.*

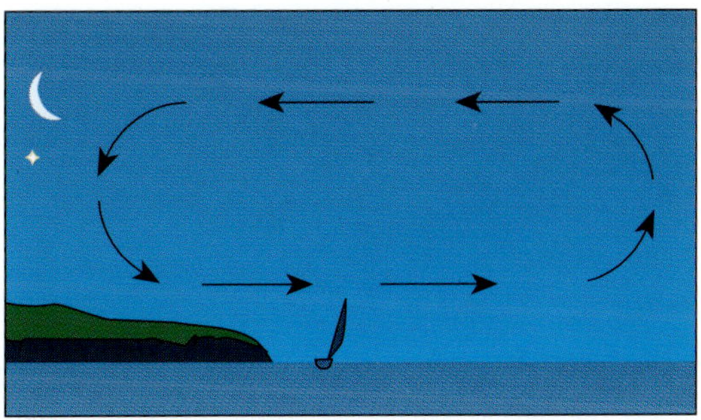

Land Breeze, *at night the process is reversed. The earth cools quickly after sunset while the sea retains its temperature and so air is drawn off the land to replace the warm air rising from over the sea.*

Katabatic winds

In areas where the coastline is more dramatic and cloudless skies at night result in radiation cooling of the land, a strong, down-slope wind can develop as air in contact with the ground becomes chilled and flows rapidly down the hillside.

Fog can form at any time of year but does so most frequently in late spring to mid-summer. It occurs when warm moist air is cooled sufficiently to become saturated and condense into water vapour.

Advection or **Sea Fog** occurs when warm moist air flows over a relatively cold sea surface and the temperature of the air in contact with this surface is lowered. If the sea temperature is below the dew point temperature of the air and cooling continues until the air is saturated, condensation will take place and form mist or fog.

Radiation or **Land Fog.** A clear night sky results in rapid cooling of the land. Should the surface temperature fall below the dew point temperature of the air, saturation will occur and condensation will take place with the formation of fog which may drift out to sea.

Beaufort wind force scale

Force	Knots	Wind	Probable Sea State
1	1-3	Light Airs	Ripples
2	4-6	Light Breeze	Small Wavelets
3	7-10	Gentle Breeze	Crests begin to break
4	11-16	Mod. Breeze	Waves becoming larger, frequent white crests
5	17-21	Fresh Breeze	Mod. waves, many white crests, some spray
6	22-27	Strong Breeze	Large waves, extensive white crests
7	28-33	Near Gale	Sea heaps up, waves breaking white foam blown in streaks
8	34-40	Gale	Mod. high waves crests break into spindrift, white foam
9	41-47	Strong Gale	High waves, crests topple spray affects visibility
10	48-55	Storm	Very high breaking waves, dense foam streaks

CAUTION Originally devised for larger sailing craft, this scale is only a rough guide to what may be expected in open water. Wind speeds are averages and gusts up to the next Force should be anticipated. Sea conditions are generally more severe nearer to land and wave height can increase dramatically within minutes.

You should never venture outside sheltered waters unless you have obtained a current weather forecast and have the ability to interpret it correctly.

Forecasts

BBC Radio Shipping Forecasts

Radio 4 198 kHz. Longwave 1515m

0033 0555 1355 and 1750

Forecasts for Inshore Waters

Radio 3 1215 kHz. 247m at 0655

Radio 4 Longwave at 0038

NOTE Broadcast times are subject to change.

Gale warnings are given at programme junctions following their issue and after each hourly news bulletin.

A gale warning indicates that winds of at least Force 8 - 34kt gusting to 43kt - are expected in the area. A Severe Gale implies winds of Force 9 with wind gusting up to 50kt. A Storm implies winds of Force 10 gusting to 60kt.

Gale warnings remain in force until cancelled or if persisting for more than 24 hours the warning is re-issued.

Wind shifts

In the Northern hemisphere a wind is said to BACK when it shifts to blow from a more anti clockwise direction and to VEER if it shifts to blow from a direction more clockwise.

Meaning of terms

Timing of Gale Warnings

IMMINENT	Within 6hrs of time of issue
SOON	6 to 12hrs
LATER	12 to 24hrs

Visibility

GOOD	More than 5 miles
MODERATE	2 to 5 miles
POOR	1100 yards to 2 miles
FOG	Less than 1100 yards

Barometric Tendency

STEADY
Change less than 0·1mb in 3hrs

RISING OR FALLING SLOWLY
Change 0·1 to 1·5mb in last 3hrs

RISING OR FALLING
Change 1·6 to 3·5mb in last 3hrs

RISING OR FALLING QUICKLY
Change 3·6 to 6·0mb in last 3hrs

RISING OR FALLING VERY RAPIDLY
Change of more than 6·0mb in last 3hrs

NOW RISING OR FALLING
Change within the last 3hrs

Speed of Movement

SLOWLY	up to 15kt
STEADILY	15 to 25kt
RATHER QUICKLY	25 to 35kt
RAPIDLY	35 to 45kt
VERY RAPIDLY	over 45kt

Measured distance

All patent logs should be checked periodically for accuracy. At a number of places on the coast marks have been set up in transit with accurately measured distances between them to enable the speed of vessels on passage to be checked *Fig 1*.

1

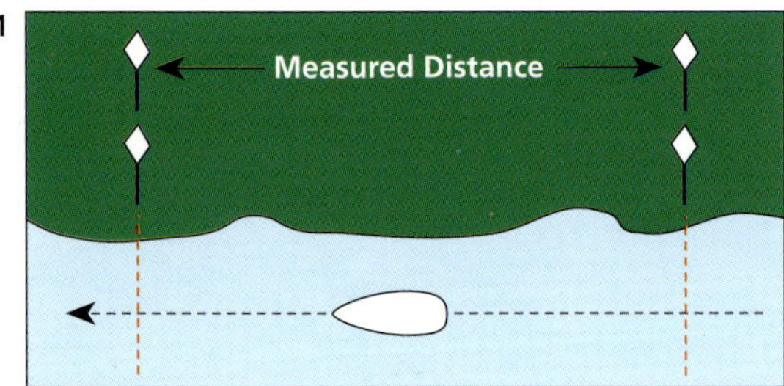

Using any charted distance of any length, steer a course at constant speed under power parallel to the chosen measured distance. Begin timing by stopwatch as the first pair of marks come into transit and stop timing at the second transit.

With only a single run past the marks allowance must be made for any tidal stream which may be affecting the course, however tidal stream can be ignored when test runs are made at identical speeds in alternate directions. In practice, when checking speed in this manner, it is customary to make two or more runs in each direction to obtain an average speed which is more dependable.

The speed of the vessel over the ground is found by dividing the distance run by the time taken.

Checking speed and distance

To check the accuracy of the Log against a measured distance

For each run made, record – Speed indicated by the log
Distance recorded by the log
Actual time taken

Complete the boxes below and compare the total distance recorded by the log for runs 1 and 2 against the measured distance to obtain the log error. Compare the average speed found against the log's recorded speed to find the log error.

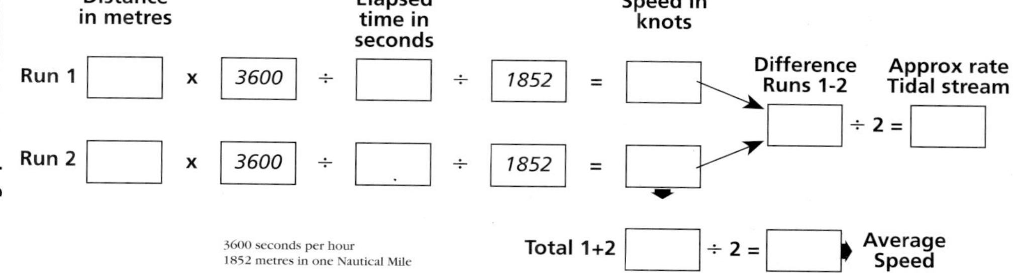

Distance in metres
Elapsed time in seconds
Speed in knots
Run 1
x 3600 ÷ ÷ 1852 =
Run 2
x 3600 ÷ ÷ 1852 =
Difference Runs 1-2
÷ 2 =
Approx rate Tidal stream
Total 1+2
÷ 2 =
Average Speed
3600 seconds per hour
1852 metres in one Nautical Mile

Time, speed, distance

$$\frac{\text{Distance x 60}}{\text{Speed}} = \text{Time}$$

$$\frac{\text{Distance x 60}}{\text{Time}} = \text{Speed}$$

$$\frac{\text{Speed x Time}}{60} = \text{Distance}$$

Time (in minutes)
Speed (in knots)
Distance (in nautical miles)

Estimated Time of Arrival (ETA)

Distance to go x 60 ÷ effective speed
= Time in mins
Add to departure time to obtain ETA

A rough estimate of boat speed can be obtained by noting the time it takes to travel its own length past a stationary object in the water.

$$\text{Speed in Knots} = \frac{\text{Length in metres}}{\text{Time in seconds}} \text{ x } 1.94$$

OR

$$\text{Speed in Knots} = \frac{\text{Length in feet}}{\text{Time in seconds}} \text{ x } 0.59$$

Tidal Stream – Computation of rate

$$\frac{\text{Range of tide for day}}{\text{Spring range of tide}} \text{ x Spring rate of tidal stream}$$

Distance off by Vertical Sextant Angle

$$\text{Dist. Off (n. miles)} = \frac{1.852 \times \text{ht. in metres}}{\text{angle in mins of arc}}$$

One Nautical Mile	=	1·852 Kilometres
	=	1·15078 Statute Miles
	=	6076·12 Feet
	=	1852 Metres
	=	10 Cables

Conversion Factors

Feet to Metres	multiply by	0·3048
Metres to Feet	"	3·2808
N Miles to St Miles	"	1·1515
St Miles to N Miles	"	0·8684
Knots to MPH	"	1·1515
MPH to Knots	"	0·8684
Knots to Km/Hr	"	1·8519
Km/Hr to Knots	"	0·5400
Sq ft to Sq m	"	0·0929
Sq m to Sq ft	"	10·7643

Apparent Movement of the Sun

1° in 4 mins

15° in 1 hour

360° in 24 hours

dist. in miles	10	20	30	40	50	60	70	80	90	100
	height in metres									
	vertical angle									
0.1	3° 05′	6° 10′	9° 12′	12°11′	15°06′	17°56′	20° 42′	23° 21′	25° 54′	28° 21′
0.2	1 33	3 05	4 38	6 10	7 41	9 12	10 42	12 11	13 39	15 06
0.3	1 02	2 04	3 05	4 07	5 08	6 10	7 11	8 11	9 12	10 12
0.4	0 46	1 33	2 19	3 05	3 52	4 38	5 24	6 10	6 55	7 41
0.5	0 37	1 14	1 51	2 28	3 05	3 42	4 19	4 56	5 33	6 10
0.6	0 31	1 02	1 33	2 04	2 34	3 05	3 36	4 07	4 38	5 08
0.7	0 27	0 53	1 19	1 46	2 12	2 39	3 05	3 32	3 58	4 24
0.8	0 23	0 46	1 10	1 33	1 56	2 19	2 42	3 05	3 28	3 52
0.9	0 21	0 41	1 02	1 22	1 43	2 04	2 24	2 45	3 05	3 26
1.0	0 19	0 37	0 56	1 14	1 33	1 51	2 10	2 28	2 47	3 05
1.1	0 17	0 34	0 51	1 07	1 24	1 41	1 58	2 15	2 32	2 49
1.2	0 15	0 31	0 46	1 02	1 17	1 33	1 48	2 04	2 19	2 34
1.3	0 14	0 29	0 43	0 57	1 11	1 26	1 40	1 54	2 08	2 23
1.4	0 13	0 27	0 40	0 53	1 06	1 19	1 33	1 46	1 59	2 12
1.5	0 12	0 25	0 37	0 49	1 02	1 14	1 27	1 39	1 51	2 04
1.6	0 12	0 23	0 35	0 46	0 58	1 10	1 21	1 33	1 44	1 56
1.7	0 11	0 22	0 33	0 44	0 55	1 05	1 16	1 27	1 38	1 49
1.8	0 10	0 21	0 31	0 41	0 52	1 02	1 12	1 22	1 33	1 43
1.9	0 10	0 20	0 29	0 39	0 49	0 59	1 08	1 18	1 28	1 38
2.0	0 09	0 19	0 28	0 37	0 46	0 56	1 05	1 14	1 23	1 33
2.1	0 09	0 18	0 27	0 35	0 44	0 53	1 02	1 11	1 19	1 28
2.2	0 08	0 17	0 25	0 34	0 42	0 51	0 59	1 07	1 16	1 24
2.3	0 08	0 16	0 24	0 32	0 40	0 48	0 56	1 05	1 13	1 21
2.4	0 08	0 15	0 23	0 31	0 39	0 46	0 54	1 02	1 10	1 17
2.5	0 07	0 15	0 22	0 30	0 37	0 45	0 52	0 59	1 07	1 14
2.6	0 07	0 14	0 21	0 29	0 36	0 43	0 50	0 57	1 04	1 11
2.7	0 07	0 14	0 21	0 27	0 34	0 41	0 48	0 55	1 02	1 09
2.8	0 07	0 13	0 20	0 27	0 33	0 40	0 46	0 53	1 00	1 06
2.9	0 06	0 13	0 19	0 26	0 32	0 38	0 45	0 51	0 58	1 04
3.0	0 06	0 12	0 19	0 25	0 31	0 37	0 43	0 49	0 56	1 02
3.1	0 06	0 12	0 18	0 24	0 30	0 36	0 42	0 48	0 54	1 00
3.2	0 06	0 12	0 17	0 23	0 29	0 35	0 41	0 46	0 52	0 58
3.3	0 06	0 11	0 17	0 22	0 28	0 34	0 39	0 45	0 51	0 56
3.4	0 05	0 11	0 16	0 22	0 27	0 33	0 38	0 44	0 49	0 55
3.5	0 05	0 11	0 16	0 21	0 27	0 32	0 37	0 42	0 48	0 53
3.6	0 05	0 10	0 15	0 21	0 26	0 31	0 35	0 41	0 46	0 52
3.7	0 05	0 10	0 15	0 20	0 25	0 30	0 35	0 40	0 45	0 50
3.8	0 05	0 10	0 15	0 20	0 24	0 29	0 34	0 39	0 44	0 49
3.9	0 05	0 10	0 14	0 19	0 24	0 29	0 33	0 38	0 43	0 48
4.0	0 05	0 09	0 14	0 19	0 23	0 28	0 32	0 37	0 42	0 46
4.1	0 05	0 09	0 14	0 18	0 23	0 27	0 32	0 35	0 41	0 45
4.2	0 04	0 09	0 13	0 18	0 22	0 27	0 31	0 35	0 40	0 44
4.3	0 04	0 09	0 13	0 17	0 22	0 26	0 30	0 35	0 39	0 43
4.4	0 04	0 08	0 13	0 17	0 21	0 25	0 30	0 34	0 38	0 42
4.5	0 04	0 08	0 12	0 16	0 21	0 24	0 29	0 33	0 37	0 41
4.6	0 04	0 08	0 12	0 16	0 20	0 24	0 28	0 32	0 36	0 40
4.7	0 04	0 08	0 12	0 16	0 20	0 24	0 28	0 32	0 36	0 39
4.8	0 04	0 08	0 12	0 15	0 19	0 23	0 27	0 31	0 35	0 39
4.9	0 04	0 08	0 11	0 15	0 19	0 23	0 27	0 30	0 34	0 38
5.0	0 04	0 07	0 11	0 15	0 19	0 22	0 25	0 30	0 33	0 37
	32.8	65.6	98.41	31.2	164.0	196.8	229.7	262.5	295.3	328.1
	height in feet									

See page 82